"The best book about how and why to interview your parents? Yes. But I was not expecting his own stories to be so fascinating, too. Couldn't stop reading start-to-finish."

—DEREK SIVERS, AUTHOR OF ANYTHING YOU WANT

"While talking with adults in therapy or everyday life, you can feel the weight of what's been unsaid to their parents: the questions they wish they'd asked, the words they wish they'd said. And often now it's too late. So I am delighted by One Last Question Before You Go, full of deep insights, good humor, and practical suggestions. I wish I'd had it myself with my own parents."

—RICK HANSON, PHD, BESTSELLING AUTHOR OF BUDDHA'S BRAIN, RESILIENT, AND MAKING GREAT RELATIONSHIPS

"With wit, intelligence, and optimism, Thiermann reveals that by asking the questions we'd rather avoid and by zooming in on the events we'd rather forget, we can heal what's broken and learn to listen, forgive, and love in a much deeper way."

—ADAM SKOLNICK, AUTHOR OF AMERICAN TIGER

"I never knew my mom was once a go-go dancer in Harlem."

—MATT, READER

ONE LAST QUESTION BEFORE YOU GO

Kyle Thiermann

ONE LAST QUESTION BEFORE YOU GO

Why You Should Interview Your Parents

LIONCREST
PUBLISHING

COPYRIGHT © 2025 KYLE THIERMANN
All rights reserved.

ONE LAST QUESTION BEFORE YOU GO
Why You Should Interview Your Parents

FIRST EDITION

ISBN   978-1-5445-4980-4   *Hardcover*
       978-1-5445-4979-8   *Paperback*
       978-1-5445-4981-1   *Ebook*

Dedicated to ET, Foster, Toby, and Mom for courageously letting me tell our family's story, so other families can better tell theirs.

Gulp, here we go.

Contents

1. What was your parenting style? 11
2. What do you believe that most people think is crazy? 17
3. How do you want to die? 23
4. What advice would you give to your younger self about money? 27
5. What have you changed your mind about? 33
6. What's a helpful question you've asked yourself throughout life, and why? 41
7. What's one thing you put off for way too long? 47
8. What is the story of this photograph? 51
9. What movie influenced you most in life? 57
10. What's a belief that got you into trouble? 65
11. What is the biggest misconception about you? 71
12. What trip will you always remember? 79
13. How do you manage stress? 85
14. Describe the culture around you when you were in college. How did it influence your outlook on the world? 89

15. What's a memory that makes you cringe with embarrassment?... 95
16. Which sibling are you closest with? 99
17. What should you apologize for? 107
18. What's a hobby of yours? (past or present) 111
19. What's one lesson your parents taught you that you passed down to me? 117
20. What's one thing you wanted to do differently from your parents when you raised me? 123
21. What's one thing we have in common?................................. 127
22. Have you ever had a near-death experience? What's the story? 133
23. What's a hard truth you've had to accept?............................. 139
24. What scares you but is good for you?..................................... 143
25. What is your most painful memory? 149
26. What do you want more of from your kids?.......................... 155
27. What are you most grateful for?... 161

    Interview Checklist 167
    My Exact Podcast Setup 175
    Gratitude 177
    About the Author 181

CHAPTER 1

What was your parenting style?

IN ONE OF MY EARLIEST MEMORIES, MY MOM AND I are walking along the sidewalk in downtown Santa Cruz, past the clock tower, a stately red brick structure with an American flag at its peak and a man slouched at its base. He sat on a skateboard, cardboard sign in hand, and smelled forgotten. As we passed the man, he mumbled something in our direction, and I hid beneath her wing.

But rather than whisk me away, she pivoted toward the man, locked eyes, and said, "We don't have any money for you today, but I'm sorry you're going through a rough time."

The man nodded.

"You don't need to give money to the homeless," she told me once we were out of earshot. "But you do need to look them in the eye. These people go days without being acknowledged."

A few years later, my mom started a nonprofit called Above the Line, the first homeless teen center in the county. In Santa Cruz there is a widely held belief that if you submit to a career in something other than systemic healing, you are selfish, myopic, and should reflect on your life choices—preferably barefoot, while scanning the beach for plastic. The two most popular bumper stickers in town are *If You're Not Outraged, Then You're Not Paying Attention!* and a Santa Cruz Skateboards logo of a blue screaming hand. In both cases, the bumper stickers are shouting.

While not a shouter, my mom earned her degree from Berkeley during the Vietnam War, and when she moved the seventy miles south to Santa Cruz, she fit nicely into the culture of grassroots activism. She would walk into local hair salons wearing a nineties blazer, boots, and dangly earrings, and amid the aroma of hairspray and gossip, explain to women that kids were sleeping on sidewalks. Then, leaving a stack of pamphlets, she would strut out the door and catch a breath of briny coastal air. "Women don't go to the salon for perms," she once said, a glint of mischief in her eyes. "We go for therapy. When our therapist tells us to do something, we listen."

Donations poured in.

Her charm wasn't limited to salons. She once met Kelly Slater at an ayahuasca retreat and apparently had such an effect on the eleven-time Surfing World Champion that he mailed her a box of shells he collected while strolling a beach in South Africa. *Why don't you send ME a box of shells, Kelly Slater? What the fuck!*

Rounding her fourth divorce, with three of her own kids, about a million stepkids from previous marriages, and a city of homeless minors who now considered her a surrogate mom, she had a remarkable ability to stay present with her youngest, a feral beast who left teeth marks on her forearms.

"As soon as you could crawl," she told me, "you would paw at the door like a puppy. And when I held you in my arms, you demanded to face out."

Teachers tried to medicate me. My mom talked to me.

She treated my fidgets by putting a skateboard in my hand and a helmet on my head, which I proudly wore because, according to her, "Cool kids wear helmets."

By the time I was ten, I could launch sky-high from a half-pipe. Four snapped wrists later, I swapped concrete for water and set my sights on Mavericks, a famous big wave spot north of town, where waves lurch to the size of six-story buildings, and wipeouts can push a surfer so deep underwater, the alveoli in their lungs rupture, and they resurface coughing blood.

Beyond my inherent desire to break bones and sound barriers, social norms tortured me. I either struggled to make eye contact with people or locked in with intensity, earning me the middle school nickname Kyle Stareman. My older brother Toby once called me "a racehorse with blinders on." Equal parts focused and oblivious.

When I started junior high, a new school with older kids where I would be exposed to the influences our surf culture was known for—fistfights and meth—she offered me a deal: "If you don't do drugs until you're eighteen, I will pay for a trip anywhere in the world." Dreams of cobalt-blue Indonesian barrels inspired my binder doodles, and I weighed my options.

"Deal." We shook on it.

Friends were baffled that I wouldn't lie and cash in on the trip. "How's she gonna know?" they asked. Lying barely occurred to me. I respected her. She respected me.

By high school, friends started smoking mole hits, a tobacco and weed combo that you inhale through a bong. Early morning surfs were replaced with late-night partying. Clear eyes faded to vacant stares. The surf culture I grew up in was seedy, dark, and endlessly intimidating. The San Lorenzo River bifurcates Santa Cruz between the Eastside and the Westside. These localized districts exist only twenty minutes apart but may as well be in different countries. Each had its own strictly defined rules from spot to spot. Eastsiders wore blue. Westsiders wore red. I was born in the Midtown, a thin green line between these two territories, and was one of the few kids who surfed both sides of town.

Despite this, rites of passage were part of the sport, and if you didn't catch a "grom beating" every now and then, it meant you were still an outsider, unworthy of initiation. "Dunkings" were a staple. In the frigid, fifty-degree water, a forty-year-old man would grab you by the neck of the wetsuit, hold you underwater, and give you the gift of cold exposure therapy long before it was cool. If it was a slow day, he'd peel your wetsuit down to your waist. Once, in the doldrums of summer, a group of friends hog-tied me with duct tape, placed me in a blow-up raft, hoisted me over their heads like a pig on a spit, and paddled me out to the kelp beds to cook for a while.

Mothers reading this may be shaking their heads in horror, but I firmly believe my childhood was preferable to being coddled. Hazing gave me belonging. But the line got blurry between hometown pride and entitled shithead, and for way too many of my peers, it was a path that led straight to drug addiction. Crystal meth ran through our town like a wildfire. At its high point in the early 2000s, the majority of local pro surfers being paid by commercial sponsors were fully addicted, climbing into wetsuits with gaunt chests, pocked faces, and sticker-plastered surfboards from billion-dollar brands.

"Make good decisions," my mom hollered as I ran out the door at 10:00 p.m., wearing a backward hat, Vans shoes, high socks, and an extra-large T-shirt like a tent over my scrawny frame. Mostly I did, holding to our drug-free pact through a miasma of smoke and, later, OxyContin, that crippled a generation. She gave me freedom, and I took her trust seriously. She was wise enough to know that punishment would only create distance, and throughout my teens, we had an open line of communication. When I lost my virginity, I proudly told her I wore a condom.

CHAPTER 2

What do you believe that most people think is crazy?

ONE YEAR AGO, MY MOM WAS WALKING BACKWARD IN A PARKing garage, helping a friend reverse her car out of a tight spot. Distracted, she stepped in the path of the garage lever—the thing that lifts up when you pay to leave—and the metal bar came crashing down on her head. She raised her hands, but the force of the lever drove her to the ground, fracturing her left hip and femur.

Each year, about 350,000 Americans fall and break a hip. Of those, 20 percent never walk again. For the elderly, a broken hip is often the first domino toward death. Moving hurts, so they become sedentary, and the dominoes start to fall.

My mom had always been spry. She hiked, swam, and blended vegetables from her garden into smoothies, so it was unsettling to see her with a cane. When dogs approached, she'd grip the nearest wall as if shaken by an earthquake. A brush with death can inspire strange responses, and after the accident, she became the Marie Kondo of mortality, organizing a packet with passwords to her accounts, a list of people to notify after she died, a photo album of her life, music that touched her, and a letter to her family. She also toured cemeteries with Foster, her husband of more than twenty years. One potential grave site was on a verdant bluff overlooking the Northern California sea.

"We laid down in the grass to see how it felt," she said.

I imagined my mom and stepdad in the cemetery, lying on their backs like they were testing mattresses at Bed Bath & the Great Beyond.

"But if there's one place we won't be able to enjoy the view," she added, "it's from six feet under the dirt." Ultimately, they decided on a cemetery in Santa Cruz, in a shaded redwood grove next to the largest homeless encampment in town.

My mom may have been sanguine about the prospect of her own demise, but when I saw her hobbling around, frail as a bird, I slid into a bad mood that lasted for weeks. Slight annoyances ballooned into existential meltdowns. As days passed, my edge sharpened into bitter resentment, aimed at the person who had supported me most in the world: my mom.

In recent years, conspiracy theories had forced our relationship into a game of Operation. We navigated holidays cautiously, careful not to zap ourselves with the wrong subject. Occasionally, we would engage in a nice little email war. She'd fire off a few links that ranged from lacking context to completely insane. I'd send her sources that had been "bought and paid for," and we'd call it a day.

It was a slow creep from antiwar hippie to conspirituality: the blending of useful modalities like breath work and meditation with stranger ideas like free energy—an alternative physics theory based on the torus, a whirlpool vortex seen throughout nature. Supporters of this fringe theory believe that inventors have created perpetual motion machines by mimicking sacred geometry. These free energy devices can produce limitless energy, replace fossil fuels, and halt humanity's drunken shuffle toward oblivion. Not to be confused with solar, wind, or geothermal, free energy taps harmonic frequencies to harness an invisible field around us. Allegedly, this technology dates back to ancient Egypt. Crop circles are, in fact, blueprints to build free energy devices. Nikola Tesla was involved, and it has been subject to a centuries-long suppression campaign enforced by the Illuminati.

My mom and stepdad have spent the last twenty years making feature-length documentaries and investing millions of dollars into this conspiracy theory, among many others.

Thanks to the algorithm, conspiracies spread like spiderweb cracks on a windshield. One turns to two, then five, then twelve. The epistemological mortar that binds them is the idea of an ominous *They*—puppet masters who pull the strings of disparate global events. It's hard to overstate the impact of social media on the human brain and family dynamics. Until its inception, most people mostly agreed on basic facts. Walter Cronkite, widely known as the most trusted voice in America during the 1960s, finished his segments with a tagline emblematic of the times: "And that's the way it is." Not anymore. Now when my mom and I look up at the same blue sky, she sees chemtrails, where I see clouds.

Some of you will take issue with my cavalier use of the term *conspiracy theorist*, as this hex can be used to discredit whistleblowers who turn out to be legit. So let's be clear: Some conspiracies are real. Tobacco companies knew that cigarettes cause cancer, but for years, they *conspired* to hide this from customers. Governments lie. Gulf of Tonkin. Iraq's weapons of mass destruction. MK Ultra. *Look into it, man!*

My critique is less about any single conspiracy theory and

more about the worldview its adherents adopt. Today, a sprawling movement of baby boomers reject traditional journalism as a matter of principle. They conflate acknowledging expertise with appealing to authority. Confirmation bias is the tendency to favor information that confirms one's beliefs and is difficult to dislodge once affirmed. Pareidolia is the tendency to see patterns in randomness. I believe my mom, stepdad, and scores of other septuagenarians are victims of both. (They'd say the same about me.) But no matter your politics, religion, or thoughts on the Illuminati, you probably have some version of this in your own parents. We all disagree about *something*, and relationships drift apart without effort. Rather than confront our parents, which seems to be all the rage among millennials, asking about the stories of their lives is a bit more zen.

This is your permission to play journalist. Consider it a vacation from the worldwide obsession with moving our mouths to make noise.

Interviewing your parents is like a psychedelic trip—helpful for most, life-changing for some—but not for everyone. There's a thin line between difficult and damaging, and only you can make that call. If this were an Rx infomercial, right about now is where a disclaimer would appear on the lower part of the screen, and the narrator would hastily say, "Check with a doctor to see if interviewing your parents is right for you."

Even if interviewing your parents isn't in the cards, I hope the thoughts I share in this book can apply to others in your life: grandparents, friends, siblings, or community members. That said, I'm not going to pretend that interviewing your parents is the same as interviewing a buddy. It's not. Chances are, you are living in response to your parents: Either you want to be like them or you want to be nothing like them.

We tend to have concretized opinions of our parents, like

statues locked in time. Questions are a tool to soften and remold these figures with more nuance, detail, and grace. And if you record the project, you will create digital family heirlooms to pass down through the generations.

I have been recording podcasts weekly since 2017, and I've learned techniques that can make any interview run more smoothly. But I don't know your parents, and the way I fumbled through my process might not apply to your life. Some of my attempts failed gloriously. I share these awkward situations because interviewing our parents is messy business, and sometimes shit goes off the rails.

I also burn some calories on my own upbringing. In this way, a few parts may feel like memoir masquerading as how-to. Relax. I promise you'll get everything you need to nail an expertly crafted interview. (If you get antsy, flip to the back to see a bullet-point list of practical advice that I weave through the story. Refer to this list when you call your parents and do the thing.)

I also talked to experts in memory, psychology, and parent–child dynamics. A few concepts—like the difference between emotional memory and factual memory—may clarify why your parents remember some stories while others recede like the tide.

After my mom's accident, I was forced to reckon with the fact that if she had died, her stories would have died with her. She had survived the sixties, launched nonprofits, produced films, traveled, married, divorced, and raised kids. I didn't want the evidence of her life to be limited to photographs and fading memories. I didn't want her stories to remain a mystery because I didn't take the time to ask.

CHAPTER 3

How do you want to die?

"ASK HER HOW SHE WANTS TO DIE," MY FRIEND RACHEL ANTIcoli suggested as we brainstormed questions for my mom over Thai food. "Most people don't think about it until it's too late." (Rachel was also in Episode 278 of my podcast.)

She pointed her chopsticks at me and slurped down curry the color of blood. Rachel is a hospice nurse and the happiest person I know. She has curly blonde hair, sun-kissed cheeks, and a laugh that spirals upward like a tornado, sucking bystanders into it with her.

"I remember being with one man on his deathbed," she said. "On his last day, his wife showed up dressed in lingerie. It's what he wanted." As I conjured the image, I wondered if the couple's children were present, too. If witnessing their father's death didn't traumatize them, their mother's striptease sure would.

Rachel's friends call her the Reaper. Fitting, as she believes that each of us should think through death before the big shebang. We all know it's going to happen, so why not confront it? Go out on our terms. And when that day finally arrives, make sure it's the best death ever.

To qualify for hospice, two doctors must agree that the patient has less than six months to live. That's when Rachel comes in. She visits homes or assisted living facilities, educates the family on their options, and asks a lot of questions.

"I remember one death. The woman had throat cancer, so she couldn't drink the end-of-life medication."

"Did you use an IV?" I mumbled through a mouthful of pad see ew.

"No, she inserted it into her rectum. Like a Push Pop." I slurped down the noodles.

"It was just this woman, her husband, and me. She held the Push Pop out like a champagne toast and said, 'Goodbye, my loves!' When she pushed it up her rectum, I watched her face turn whitish purple. The color moved down her whole body, and then she died. It was the most amazing death I've ever seen." She rested her chin on her hand and gazed dreamily out the window as streaks of rain wept across the glass.

Rachel worked in trauma care for twelve years prior to hospice. One day, after a shift that ended at eight o'clock in the morning, she walked to a beach near her home and collapsed in the sand.

"Every day, I was trying to keep people from dying. I was like, I'm a superhero, I'll keep you alive no matter what, but it sort of felt like a lie. Sometimes dying really is the best option."

Asking about taboo subjects like death, sex, or money can feel weird, but they are invitations to intimacy. Tension is necessary for any good interview, so if you feel your chest tighten or stutter midway through a question, you might be on the right track. Derek Sivers (Episode 386), an entrepreneur and philosopher, put it this way:

My grandfather was on his deathbed, so I went to see him. But the whole time, I had this big, unaskable question in my head: "What's it like to know you're about to die?" Finally, I got the courage. He had been falling in and out of sleep, but as soon as I asked, his face lit up and he said, "It's wonderful. Every baby born is going to die, and everything else in my life has been great, so I think this will be great too. I'm excited." And then he fell asleep and died the next day. I was really glad I asked that too-bold, too-rude question. I make a habit of doing that now.

Back at dinner with Rachel, I tried this approach.

"How do you want to die?" I asked.

"I want to die in one of those flying suit things." She held her arms in a T shape.

"Squirrel suits?"

"Yes, those! I want to jump off a big cliff and just, you know… not make it. Splat!" She clapped her hands together.

"Splat," I repeated absently. "How old do you want to be?"

"Fifty."

"Fifty?" I said, first confused, then mad. For such a high-altitude death, I told her she may be setting her sights a bit low and asked that she please push it back a few decades. We need the Reaper to have a long, healthy life before turning the scythe on herself. She yawned and said she couldn't make any promises.

"I want to go out on my terms," she said. "No hospitals, no tubes."

I asked Rachel if she noticed any themes around how people die. Why do some confront it with gusto while others live in denial until their final day?

She said simply, "People die the way they live."

CHAPTER 4

What advice would you give to your younger self about money?

THE INITIAL SPARK FOR THIS PROJECT STARTED TWO YEARS before my mom broke her hip. It was a blustery spring morning, and I recorded a podcast with a charismatic old hound, who also happened to be my dad (Episode 204).

My dad's name is Eric, but everyone calls him ET. Ironic as he's the parent who's never given much mind to life on other planets.

We did the podcast in my home at the time, a 1997 Ford RV named Starflyte. It had teal carpet, white polka-dot curtains, silver dish rims, and the collapsible table behind the driver's seat tripled as my office, kitchen, and podcast studio.

ET had deep smile lines that webbed his face and skin that hung off his Adam's apple like a stalactite. He wore oval spectacles and a surf hat that I had gifted him. He likes keeping up with the latest styles and figures the best way to stay cool is through his kid's hand-me-downs.

...Hand-me-ups?

"I bet you've interviewed more people than I have," I said as I fiddled with the knobs on my Zoom PodTrak P4 recorder. The whole setup fit in my backpack, and the base of the microphone was worn from the hands of big wave surfers, hunters, psychedelics researchers, environmental activists, porn stars, authors, astrophysicists, and now, the man who gave me life.

"I probably *have* interviewed more people than you," ET said, inching himself closer to the microphone. "But you're catching up." ET has a graying widow's peak, rusty irises, and a habit of sniffling before speaking during allergy season. As a career filmmaker, good audio was a maxim in our household.

Keep your friends close and your microphones closer.

"Ready?"

"Ready, Freddie." He laced his hands around an insulated Yeti coffee mug, dirt from his yard wedged beneath his fingernails.

I scanned my notebook one last time, snapped it closed, and started the interview. "Tell the story of Muhammad Ali and the mirror."

He tilted his head, chuckled, and found the memory in the attic of his mind.

I start most of my podcasts with a question that will get a laugh. Secret hobbies or funny stories set the tone for a delightful conversation. If you can get your parents to talk about a subject they have a positive relationship with or know a great deal about, it's like riding a bike with a cool breeze at your back. The whole trip is easier.

"That must've been in 1995," ET said. He was hired to shoot an Apple event in Palo Alto that Muhammad Ali attended. The fighter already had Parkinson's, but he loved being around people and he loved doing silly magic tricks.

"Not silly," ET corrected himself. "They were wonderful."

Before he recorded the interview with Ali, ET walked up to the fighter and revealed a small mirror from his pocket.

"Take a look at yourself," ET said. Ali held the mirror in his shaking hand and put it to his face. The mirror laughed at him. *Ha, ha, ha, ha, ha!* It was a gag.

"You could've heard a pin drop in the room." ET smirked. "And Ali, he just cracked up." My dad gifted the mirror to Muhammad Ali, who spent the rest of the day walking up to high-paid Apple executives and holding the mirror to their smug faces.

"What's your relationship with the Santa Cruz Flea Market?" I pivoted.

"It's the land of opportunity," he said, taking a sip of coffee. "It's modern-day treasure hunting."

Over the past thirty years, ET has barely missed a weekend. Sometimes, he'll find a treasure at the Flea, a pet iguana or vacuum-powered hair clipper, bargain with the seller to the bitter end, and then pay the original asking price. Talk about a love of the game. A friend once got him a card that read, "To the man who has everything...and keeps it all in his garage." ET probably saved the card.

Despite being in his seventies, ET still believes that speed is his greatest asset, always scheming clever ways he can shave off a few seconds here and there. Why waste time brushing your teeth in the bathroom when your center console is a perfectly good place for a toothbrush? Gillette razor in the glove box? What a hack! This is all well and good until ET texts us kids photos of himself forty feet up a ladder precariously pitched against a eucalyptus tree, chain saw in hand. His commitment to moving fast is part of a grander philosophy that if he maintains velocity, he'll outrun time itself and start getting younger. "As soon as you slow down, you are slowing down," ET likes to say.

Sometimes, ET's inner didact will come out, and he'll deliver moral instruction with urgency.

"Did I ever tell you the story of Joseph Heller?" he'll say.

"Yeah, a bun—"

"So Heller wrote the wildly popular book *Catch-22*. He's at a billionaire's house on Shelter Island, and his pal Kurt Vonnegut informs Heller that their host, a hedge fund manager, makes more money in a day than Heller did on his entire novel. Heller responds, 'But I have something he will never have.' Do you know what that is?"

"Enough," we'll both mouth.

During the podcast in Starflyte, new stories spilled out of ET like a cracked dam that needs only a thimble to break. Unprompted, he told me about his philosophies on creativity: "The best projects come from volunteering." Health: "I have friends who are in their seventies. All they do is complain about their bodies. Fuck that. Is that all you have to talk about? What a waste of time. Get over it. Move on." And money: "Whether you're making ten bucks an hour or ten million an hour, you got problems. The real trick is to become someone who is fun to play with. Do that, and you'll be okay." He also told the story of his own father, who lost his retirement at age ninety in the 2008 Bernie Madoff scandal and was forced to go back to work as a supermarket greeter for ten bucks an hour. Despite this tragedy, ET still thinks of cash like avocados—best to give it away before it rots. "I like living close to the bone," he growled. "Keeps me hungry."

Over the course of an hour, I learned more about my dad than I had in the ten years prior. The podcast allowed me to ask questions that might otherwise have been too awkward and lock into undistracted time that was rare. The next day, I received this email.

Hi Kyle,

Thank you for recording the interview with me. Made me feel like what I had to say was important. I think a lot of parents feel disappointed that their children aren't more interested in them, in their colorful history, or how they think about the world. Relationships are improved by careful listening.

Okay, my friend, you know the drill. Take what inspires, leave the rest in the dung heap.

Over and out.

xoET

Viral is a strong word, but for my little corner of the internet, the podcast was very popular. In the following weeks, I received dozens of emails from listeners who picked up their phones and interviewed their own parents. One listener named Ian from Montana wrote, "I just listened to your podcast with your dad and became motivated enough to interview both of my parents individually. Wow, I feel such a weight lifted from my chest! These recordings have become my most valuable possessions."

I was energized by the response, but the prospect of sitting down with my mom and stepdad was another story, and I waited another two years—when my mom broke her hip—to take the next step.

CHAPTER 5

What have you changed your mind about?

MY FOLKS SPLIT UP WHEN I WAS SIX. THE CREATIVE CHAOS that was ET didn't match with my mom's trains-run-on-time mentality. After the divorce, they agreed to never talk shit about each other in front of me. Not until years later did I learn that divorce was synonymous with failed marriages. A few years after their divorce, my mom met a man at an environmental summit, and by the time I was eleven, I had a new parental figure in my life. Foster Gamble had thinning white hair, spoke in a radio-clear voice, and wore purple most days of the week. A former Division I hockey player and aikido black belt, he was sturdy with a square jaw and confident as a crack of thunder.

Early into their relationship, Foster drove me to a San Jose Sharks hockey game, a first for me. When players banged into the plexiglass, we spilled popcorn and laughed.

"Kyle," he said on our drive home. "I love your mom, but I'm not trying to replace your dad." My defenses melted.

If you can't interview your biological *parents*, I urge you to use the word more elastically. Because across history, the nuclear family has been a thing for about two minutes. In the book *Sex at Dawn*, Christopher Ryan, PhD, and Cacilda Jethá showed that partible paternity was a common belief among foraging societies—the idea that a fetus emerges from multiple biological fathers whose semen collects in the mother's womb over time. Although this theory doesn't jibe with our modern understanding of how the bun gets baked, it served a critical evolutionary function for these tribes. The role of fatherhood was shared among each man who contributed his...ingredients, ensuring paternal protection of the child. Hawaii has a history of partible paternity called *poʻolua*, and King Kamehameha I, conqueror and first ruler of the Kingdom of Hawaii, was said to have had two fathers. Even today, the net of family is cast liberally across the Polynesian islands, where the elderly are affectionately referred to as "aunties" and "uncles."

"If you were raised by one or two parents, you have a built-in assumption that that's where love comes from," said Ryan (Episode 331). "But what if a kid has three mothers or five fathers? How does that affect their expectations of where love comes from? It's the difference between being raised under a sky full of stars or a sky with just one moon. You see the universe differently." Like waves to Hawaiians, the definition of *parent* can carry a constellation of nuance. Interview anyone who feels like a parent to you—a title not defined by genes but by the ones who showed up.

In addition to interviewing my biological dad, ET, I also sat down with Foster as he was a formative figure in my childhood; I consider him a dad.

Foster came from old money. He is the great-great-grandson of James Gamble, of Procter & Gamble, and a few years after courting my mom, they moved into a mansion in the Santa

Cruz mountains. It was the nicest place I had ever seen. The deck out front had a spanning view of Monterey Bay, complete with a pool, at-home gym, and massage chair made by Ferrari. Expansive windows along the southern wall gave the feeling of being encased in glass, and when the marine layer blanketed the coast on summer mornings, they felt the sun, hawks swooping at eye level, living above the clouds.

And there was the library room, filled with hundreds of books and binders from floor to ceiling. Topics included crop circles, Illuminati, chemtrails, and the global domination agenda.

By the time my mom and Foster got together, he was already enthusiastic about some fairly strange ideas. Most notably, free energy. Foster was bankrolling a number of inventors who claimed to have built perpetual-motion devices by mimicking "cosmic vortices with copper coils that create toroidal fields," according to Foster's blog. The Second Law of Thermodynamics states that any spontaneously occurring process will always lead to an escalation in entropy. In other words, ice cubes melt, people age, and perpetual-motion machines don't exist. But Foster believes that "Physics has ignored half of the universe! A torus is not a closed or isolated system. It is open to the rest of the universe, as are galaxies, solar systems and the atoms that provide the electricity in our very own bodies." Foster talked with several people who had "very authentic sounding reports of having been on extra-terrestrial spacecrafts. They each talked independently of a toroidal drive centering the ship."

In front of Foster's house sits a fountain, custom-built and ornately tiled, royal purple and Tiffany blue. A goblet protrudes from the center, sucking water up the stem. The water swirls clockwise in the giant chalice before spilling down the sides to form a miniature whirlpool. Foster designed the fountain in the shape of a toroidal vortex, an homage to free energy devices and the pattern that allows them to function.

The house primarily runs on solar, just to be clear.

My mom had wrapped up a decade of work with homeless teens and was looking for her next thing. That next thing turned out to be Thrive, a media company that pushed conspiracy theories to the masses. Thrive spawned two feature-length documentaries, created and cohosted by my mom and Foster. The first film, they claim, is the "most-viewed independent documentary ever." It's on YouTube. Knock yourself out.

The film is difficult to describe, as it attempts to tackle more subjects than any story ever should. But if there were a thread, it's that aliens have given us the blueprints of free energy by way of crop circles, and inventors have used these cosmic instructions to build devices that can power cities by harmonizing with the abundant energy of the universe. Foster believes that he was given a vision of free energy while riding a school bus as a child, and his life's purpose is to expose the elite cabal suppressing it and shepherd free energy to the world.

* * *

When I met Foster, my two grand ambitions were to become a pro surfer and hit puberty before high school. But when I learned about free energy, my brain cracked wide open, and I, too, proselytized the good gospel to anyone who would listen. Free energy made me feel cool—Secret Agent Kyle—part of an inner circle that would upend the future as we knew it. The idea that a guy like me could change the world was incredibly seductive. Conspiracy spoke to my yearning for uniqueness, and it was a way to connect with my mom and Foster. Together, we watched David Icke documentaries and read Alex Jones articles aloud. They were never pushy about it. I *wanted* to learn. We talked about big ideas. The best drug on earth.

My junior year of high school, I transferred to a homeschool program. My mom, Foster, and I were excited about the idea, but my biological dad, ET, was concerned.

"Who's gonna teach him algebra?" ET asked my mom. "Who's gonna teach him Shakespeare?" But there was no time for *Hamlet*. Not with the Illuminati closing in.

"Do you think it's important to learn Shakespeare?" my mom asked me. Of course I didn't, and it was settled. ET never had a chance.

By the time I was sixteen, I was pursuing pro surfing in earnest, and homeschool let me schedule my days around the tides. In the obsidian predawn light, I would paddle out in glacier-clear water, shadowed by Monterey's white sand dunes. "Goooo!" a photographer named Chachi would screech from the impact zone, holding his camera encased in a waterproof housing. I'd pull into a heaving blue barrel (where the wave surrounds a surfer completely) and strike a nonchalant pose. He'd reach his arm through the wave and snap a burst of shots before the foamy vortex closed out. If the photo ran in a magazine, my sponsor, Sector 9 Skateboards, would keep paying me $300 a month. "I remember the first shot we ever got in a magazine," said Chachi. "You were honestly bummed. Your stance wasn't as stylish as you hoped, so you couldn't even celebrate the win." Compared to peers, who seem to have the genetics of Cirque du Soleil performers, I always felt off balance and one step behind. I was a small kid with hollow bird bones for arms, a blond afro, and a coltish style that resembled a mild seizure. Friends made sure I knew it. Evidence of my mediocrity caused me to spiral, as deep down, I knew I was chasing my passion—not my talent. But what I lacked in agility, I made up for in self-loathing and monomania. It was an engine, albeit a dirty one. Given the sheer quantity of hours I spent in salt water each week, it would have been hard *not* to improve. My mom made me treat surfing like a class. If I wanted to do it for real, I had to write sponsors, negotiate deals, and train.

Foster didn't surf himself, but he had coached athletes in a number of sports, teaching them breath control, mindset, and visualization. He offered to work with me. We would face each other, barefoot, stance like sumo wrestlers. "Hold your hands out in front of you and picture laser beams shooting out the tips of your fingers. Feel the force move up through your genitals into your heart chakra, and as this energy shoots out the crown of your head, I want you to think to yourself...*I am strong.*"

"I am strong," I mouthed. I squatted lower, pursed my lips, and let out an exhale. *I am strong.* I felt a surge of virility. It was the first time I had consciously directed the spotlight of my attention to think a positive thought. My toes curled on his pearl rug, mind rippling with focus.

My pivot away from compulsory education resulted in a deep well of knowledge in niche subjects—*boy, could I scare girls away with my diatribes on fractional reserve lending*—while leaving me bereft in basic math. I studied in the library room. One day, my mom and Foster taught me about the history of public schools.

"This is how it all started," Foster said, handing me a black-and-white photograph of children standing in line to enter a schoolhouse, men in uniform holding the new students at gunpoint.

"Jesus Christ!" I said, shaking my head in horror.

"The function of public school is to produce obedient cogs," Foster said. "It's by design."

I'm no cog, I thought, brow furrowed. "I'm Neo."

One night over chicken and mashed potatoes, ET voiced his concern about my education. "I just worry that you'll miss out on some important milestones," he cautioned. "There's just a base level of knowledge that can be useful later on, even if you don't see the value now."

What did he know? ET was an institutionalist, one of the sheeple. I wiped my mouth with a napkin, stood up from the table, and said, "Yeah, well, I respect Foster more than you."

ET stared at me but said nothing. He looked down, considered his mashed potatoes, and his fork met his lips. I walked to my room and slammed the door.

The Matrix was a perfect metaphor for me at that age. Guy has a small life, unplugs from the matrix, learns kung fu, and saves the world. The more conspiracy theories I downed, the more my self-worth soared. I was no longer a powerless teen. The world was no longer an achingly complex place. It was a pyramid. Everything could be traced back to the top. Unlike surfing, which takes about a decade to get the hang of, conspiracy theories promised high status with zero effort. I was a digital soldier fighting a shadow war for the fate of humanity. *I knew kung fu.*

Once, I tagged along on a trip to vet a free energy technology. We flew out to an adobe house in New Mexico, where a portly gentleman and his son guided us to their garage, unveiling an otherworldly contraption. The machine trilled to life, green lights blinking and I thought, *This is how it happens. This is exactly how history is made.* Then the garage door swung open, and in waddled their pet pig.

Wealth legitimizes ideas, no matter how misbegotten. As a teen, I would drive my dented Isuzu Rodeo to a house that required a gate code to enter, passing gardeners, house cleaners, and a pool guy on my way to the front door. I saw firsthand how

Foster's money inspired people to be 10 percent friendlier, 10 percent more likely to nod along with winning smiles as he talked about the reptilian elite. And as we sat around the dinner table, a starlit view of the bay below, and Foster spoke about free energy with booming authority, my mom by his side, I'd think, *How could it not be real? Look at all of this.* I wonder how much sooner I would have abandoned the ideas had they not been coated in gold.

CHAPTER 6

What's a helpful question you've asked yourself throughout life, and why?

LET ME TELL YOU ABOUT AN EXPERIMENT THAT PITTED A two-year-old toddler named Alia against a whip-smart bonobo named Kanzi. You may have heard of Kanzi as he's rather famous, touted on Oprah's show as the smartest bonobo in the world. Kanzi can communicate hundreds of words using lexigrams on a keyboard. Show Kanzi an egg, and the bonobo will knuckle-walk over to the keyboard, push the button for egg, and an AI voice will say, "Egg." Kanzi can also join words together. Once, while chewing a stem of raw kale, he pushed the symbols "slow" and "lettuce" to voice his frustration with the bitter vegetable. Kanzi's linguistic skills were roughly neck and neck with young Alia, outpacing her in some areas. He could even blow up a balloon, debunking the previously held assumption that nonhuman animals cannot consciously control their breathing patterns. The bonobo's confidence knew no bounds as he made a pass at journalist Lisa Ling and her scruffy cameraman—reminding us that humans aren't the only species who swing both ways.

But Alia broke away in one area: *her ability to ask a question.* While Kanzi could make requests, Alia could make requests for information. This distinction speaks to the human ability to recognize a "missing piece of knowledge," psychologist Paul Harris wrote in his book *Trusting What You're Told: How Children Learn from Others.*

* * *

I like to channel my inner toddler when writing questions, and I like to do it with a strong cup of coffee. Caffeinated toddlers are supremely confident and they will be our spirit animals for the remainder of this chapter.

Mom Interview. I wrote the words in bold letters at the top of a page, underlining them for a little extra zhuzh. My eyes yawned up to the varnished rafters, where a slanted shaft of light cut across the coffee shop.

Tap, tap, tap. Nothing.

How do you believe this bullshit? I scribbled the question, chuckled, and the smile faded as quickly as it came. I fumbled for my phone. *Instagram! That's where I'll find answers.* But as my hand found the smooth, black glass of procrastination, I remembered that I had been here before. I had a system to deal with it.

By the time I acknowledged the nagging thought that I needed to interview my mom before another parking garage lever fell from the sky, I had moved to LA to work at a creative agency, getting paid to write commercials, billboards, and taglines for companies that want you to buy their brand-new whatever. When I started, I wrote ads for an irreverent mushroom chai startup called MUD\WTR that poked fun at society's trauma bond with coffee. (I always wrote these ads while sipping a latte.) While at this startup, I learned an important lesson in creativity: It is a game of tonnage. If you need to find a great headline, don't write five; write fifty. Creativity is the most wasteful industry on Earth, but unlike plastics or fossil fuels, the more waste you produce, the more beautiful the world becomes. The same principle applies when crafting questions.

Neither your lack of brain cells nor your parents' lackluster life is paralyzing you. It's fear. Fear that your questions will be bad, the interview will fail, and your already fragile relationship will shatter as a result of reading this stupid little book. To overcome this fear, simply write bad questions.

No one will see them but you.

In the coffee shop, I *did* pull out my phone, but instead of doomscrolling Instagram, I put it on airplane mode, set a twenty-minute timer, and forced myself to write a stinky heap of questions. Some arrived as grunts and huffs, words that made me think of my mom, but the pen kept moving. About six minutes in, I saw a faint glow, a bonfire in the distance. A memory arrived; I hadn't thought of it in years.

When I was maybe seven, my mom called Gault Elementary and told my teacher I was sick. I was not sick, and she drove us the hour north to San Francisco, where we played hooky. We walked the pier and ate clam chowder in hollowed bowls made of sourdough bread, feeding leftovers to seagulls. She gave me a quarter to buy a gumball and it spun down the track like it was on a roller-coaster ride before plopping into my hand. It was a wonderful day, but it was also the first time I had ever heard my mom lie (to get me out of school). On the drive home, I asked her when lying was okay. I forget what she told me, only that it felt like a nuanced conversation. I put my shoulder blades back on the seat and felt mature. I scribbled the question. *Lying. When okay?* This transported my mind to conspiracy. *When exactly did she get captured by these ideas? Was it as soon as she met Foster? Before?* This took me to her childhood. *Did she have an honest relationship with her parents?* I wrote it down. I wondered about her friends and hobbies, childhood home, and father, who died before I was born. As the timer ticked, pages filled with mysteries.

Once your alarm sounds, turn it off quickly. Setting an alarm in a coffee shop is a weird thing to do, and you don't want to draw attention to yourself.

* * *

Charles Duhigg is an author who wrote *The Power of Habit* and later *Supercommunicators*, a book that explores how to connect with others. When I asked Duhigg if he had tips for someone who wanted to interview their parents (Episode 351) he said, "Don't just ask about the *facts* of their life. Ask how they *feel* about their lives."

Duhigg calls these Deep Questions. Deep Questions could include:

- What do you *love* most about surfing?

- Why was your trip to Africa *important* to you?

- How does painting make you *feel*?

Follow-up questions pair well with Deep Questions, and they're the secret to good interviews. While your first question may have been rehearsed, a follow-up shows that you're paying attention. If your dad tells a story about his summer as a rafting guide in the Grand Canyon, ask him to expand on the infamous rapids.

If you notice your mom laugh, fidget, sniffle, stutter, scratch her face, change her tone, or furrow her brow, these are all poker tells that she has an emotional charge around the subject. Wait until she finishes, then ask a follow-up question that delves deeper into that moment.

Follow-up questions can be as simple as *Why did you decide to do that? Can you give me an example?* or *Tell me more about [blank].*

If a question is likely to get a yes or no response, rework it and insert words like Moment, Why, and Story. When was the *moment* you decided to hitchhike to Alaska? Tell me the *story* of your first job interview. *Why* don't you love me? Eh, scratch that last one.

A lot of interviews fail because the questions are too broad. *What's the meaning of life?* Broad questions can sound profound, but they're just lazy. When assaulted with these platitudes, the mind thrashes. Your parents talk about doing good in the world and finding your bliss. They don't sound like themselves. Your job is to get your parents to tell stories about their lives, not morph into fortune cookies.

Sure, stock questions work—see chapter titles, as well as a list of bonus questions at the end of the book—but these are just meant to start you off. The best questions will be unique to your parents. They'll appreciate it, and you'll both have a better time.

If you're still struggling to write specific questions, break their lives into four chunks (childhood, young adult, adult with kids, empty nester) and write half a dozen questions for each stage. *Who did you idolize as a kid? What did your childhood house look like? Who was your first crush?* There are three quick 'n' dirty questions for childhood. Moving on.

Once you've filled three pages with questions, go back and circle your favorite fifteen. You probably won't ask more than ten. If it takes your parents five minutes to answer each one, that's fifty minutes. Tack on follow-up questions and you're already at an hour and a half!

In some of my best podcasts, I asked no more than five provocative questions, then peppered in follow-ups.

If you're unsure whether a question is "good," ask yourself:

- Is it specific?

- Am I genuinely curious?

- Does it make me a little nervous?

If you can hit two out of three, you've struck gold.

This comes with a caveat. The first few questions will dictate the tone of the interview, so don't start with anything too heavy.

I closed my notebook, three pages full of shitty questions for my mom, and walked out of the coffee shop, armpits ripe with caffeine sweat. In the harsh afternoon light, I pulled out my phone, scrolled my favorites list, and took the single most important step of the entire interview process—making the call.

CHAPTER 7

What's one thing you put off for way too long?

WHEN I WAS EIGHTEEN, I MOVED INTO AN OLD SURF SHACK a few blocks back from Pleasure Point, a surf spot that got its name thanks to a nearby brothel during Prohibition. My housemates consisted of three college students and about three million termites. We had an unspoken agreement with our landlord. He would keep the rent low, and we would never bring up our dysfunctional toilet, refrigerator, or faulty central heating system. It was a mafioso-style, *I didn't see nothin' if you didn't see nothin'* sort of relationship.

The house was sailboat-themed, detailed with a shabby wood-paneled floor and cabinet handles in the shape of miniature wooden steering wheels. When winter storms descended upon us, the house would creak and moan like a ship at sea.

Two years into living there, I was frying eggs in a down parka, when my older brother, Toby, stopped by and proclaimed, "It's colder than a witch's titty in here!" He pointed to the large heater attached to the wall in the kitchen and asked why we weren't using it.

I told him the heater was broken and argued that it wasn't even *that* cold, as misty clouds huffed from my mouth. My brother knelt down, removed the grate, fiddled with a knob, and clicked a button; the heater ignited, warm air thawing our kitchen within minutes. He stood up and said, "Your pilot light was off, bro."

Sometimes we wait years to do things that can be accomplished in minutes.

Call your parents. Tell them you've been reading this book. Promise you'll buy them a copy. Use this script if it's helpful:

"Hi, Mom, how are you doing?" This is the DMV of questions. Everybody uses it, nobody likes it.

"I was thinking about you recently (they love that) and realized I still don't know much about your life when you were my age. I'd like to sit down sometime and get a few of your stories on tape." The word "interview" can sound like an interrogation. Learning "a few stories" lowers the stakes.

If your parent is unlikely to agree to the interview, you can pull out the big guns and say, "My birthday is coming up (technically it's always coming up), and this year I'm planning to explore more of my oral family history. I'd like to include you in this project and record a few of your stories." Some parents can be sheepish about the spotlight, and this framing makes them feel like they're just part of the project, not the whole project.

If you plan to interview multiple family members, call the one who is most likely to agree first. Once they agree, you can use that social proof to get everyone else on board.

After my podcast with ET, I talked to listeners who interviewed both of their parents at the same time. This only works if they play well off each other. You can ask about a single event—like having their first kid—and get their different perspectives on it. Generally, though, I recommend interviewing them one at a time. Even in model marriages, people will subtly shift their answers to make their partner feel comfortable. Or flat-out lie. "Before your mother, I never loved a woman." *Yeah, right.*

If your parent doesn't want you to share the recording with anyone else, agree, and honor the agreement. If there are areas of their life they don't want to touch, assure them you don't need to go there.

When I called my mom, dad, and stepdad—the subjects I would interview over the course of this project—I didn't feel ready. I could fling out excuses like a blackjack dealer. But I knew that if I didn't get it on the calendar, it would never happen.

"Hi, Mom, how are you?"

"Hi!" A buoyant voice responded through my phone.

She told me that she had just returned from physical therapy, and although she was healing, she still walked with a cane. I shuddered at the image of the prosthetic socket now implanted into her pelvic bone.

"Can I record a few of your stories next time I'm back in Santa Cruz?" I asked.

I told her I wanted to hear about her college years and learn about my grandfather Richard. By giving her two things I knew would be easy for her to talk about, it made the prospect of an interview less daunting. You are not interviewing your parents about their *lives*. You are interviewing them about *moments* of their lives.

Over the course of the following year, I interviewed my

mom three times. If you have this luxury, do it. You'll go deeper. If your mom is obsessed with sewing, you could spend a whole hour on fabric grain and thread tension.

Before I dialed her number, I had a few time slots already mapped out. I like early evenings because people tend to be more emotionally open as the sun goes down. Cortisol is lowest during the evening, making us more relaxed and sociable. Think happy hour.

I told my mom the interview would take an hour but asked that she block off three. It takes a lot of mental and emotional energy to talk into a microphone, so afterward, give yourself the space to go for a night-time walk, grab a beer, or scream into a pillow—whatever is called for. Once my mom agreed to the date, I thanked her, hung up the phone, and exhaled. Then I made similar calls to Foster and ET. The dates were set.

Feel that? Pilot light is on.

CHAPTER 8

What is the story of this photograph?

WHEN I CALLED ET, I ASKED HIM TO EMAIL PHOTOGRAPHS FROM his life. Any photos from any year, as many as he could find. The purpose was threefold: First, I wanted the photos as a mnemonic device to jog his memory. Second, I knew that photos would spark another two pages of questions. When clicking through the images he sent, I kept my notebook handy, scribbling questions as they came. And third, I wanted to steep myself in his past. Even if I never asked 90 percent of the questions, I wanted options.

Once your parent agrees to the interview, ask them to send you photos from their life. You can even bring the photos to the interview, place them on the table, and prompt a story by saying, "Tell me about this photo."

The first photo that stopped me was titled "Hot Air, I have a lot of it." ET not only emailed the photos, but he named each of them. The image was taken low, looking up at a heroic man who wore landscaping gloves and was throttling the flame of a hot-air balloon.

When I was nine, ET brought home a hot-air balloon from the Flea. "They're just giving this stuff away!" he shouted out his window as he pulled up, towing a rusty trailer with a full-sized hot-air balloon. We flew it only once, the day the photo was captured. He drove me three hours to Whamobass, an exhibition on the backside of Paso Robles, a rural part of Central California with rolling hills, oak trees, and ranchlands. At first light, some aficionados took us for a float. I remember climbing into the wooden basket, the hissing flame, gaseous heat, and frigid air as we ascended into the sky. ET kept a vice grip on me as we went up, up, up with hundreds of other balloons, a sky of circus-colored teardrops across a still dawn canvas.

Only after we touched back to earth did we learn that hot-air balloons are super dangerous and require thousands of dollars per year in insurance. It has collected dust in the garage ever since.

Tell me about the hot-air balloon, I scribbled in my notebook.

ET later corrected me on the story. The hot-air balloon did not, in fact, come from the Flea but from a hitchhiker, whom he picked up in Arcada.

* * *

The next photo was accompanied by a newspaper article titled "Establishing Shots: A New Breed of Monterey Bay Area Filmmakers Shoot Old Hollywood in the Foot." The photo portrayed a smoldering man with a popped collar, camera in hand, reminiscent of a young Jeff Goldblum from *Jurassic Park*. The caption read: "Director Eric Thiermann brings *Steel Heel*, his first feature film, to the screen. It was shot entirely in Santa Cruz and Monterey Bay...Eric Thiermann has fulfilled a personal dream by making a full-length, high-action feature that sparkles with commercial viability," the reporter gushed. "Cast with local professional and amateur actors and marketed independently by its talented director."

Shortly after I was born, ET made a movie about a vigilante who rode a Harley, sabotaged environmental polluters, and fell in love with the bad guy's daughter. Steel Heel would ride around town at night and skid the heel of his boot along the street, sparks flying off the back. ET cast the local butcher as the lead.

My mom produced the film, working her magic around town. She raised money, set the schedule, and got every shooting location for free, including the police station. She got behind her husband and made his dream happen.

Sometime between finishing the script and filming, ET had a chance to get the movie backed by a legit Hollywood production house. "We like the script," the agent told him over the phone. They would find an established Hollywood actor to play the lead. It was one of those rare opportunities: funding, distribution, and a chance to catapult his career.

"I'm sorry," said ET, "but I already promised the role to someone else." The butcher.

"Are you sure?" said the agent.

Ultimately, the film didn't "sparkle with commercial viability." It had some good showings in Santa Cruz, and that was that. A few years later, ET and my mom split up. Without a producer in his corner, he struggled to get other creative projects over the finish line.

* * *

The third photo I opened was titled "Kyle ET Tripping." It depicted my dad and me standing at a pristine alpine lake in the Sierra Nevadas, his hand resting on my shoulder, pupils as wide as our smiles. Years ago, I convinced ET to take MDMA with me. We drove his van to Tahoe, parked at a trailhead, and hiked a few miles to a lake. We brought water, puffy jackets, and a bag of white powder.

"Lick your finger and swirl it in the bag," I instructed. "Like this." I licked my own snow-covered index finger, tasted the putrid sour, stuck my tongue out in disgust, and grinned, for I knew what would follow. We meandered around the lake and waited for it to kick in. While skipping stones, we ran into two young men. They had been off the grid for months, backpacking from Mexico to Washington along the Pacific Crest Trail.

"That's so incredible," ET said as they told us of their ambulatory adventures, restraining himself, just barely, from giving them a hug. As we bid the grizzled backpackers farewell, we watched the sky turn bruised violet, and ET looked down at his feet and then back at me. "I just realized I have two different shoes on." Together, we laughed—deep and full of love. We hiked back to his Sprinter van, using our cell phone lights to guide us.

"Do you have any more of that stuff?" he asked when we slid the door shut. He sat on his lifted bed, which still had treasures strewn about from the Flea. Allen wrenches. A dolly. U-Haul moving blankets to sleep on. I sat in the passenger seat, sidesaddle, and handed him the Ziploc bag of powder.

"Got any water?" he choked. I handed it to him.

His posture changed. He took a deep breath, belly rising and falling. His shoulders slumped, and his legs dangled off the lifted bed.

"It's funny," he said. "I feel like a little boy again." He handed the water back to me.

"You remember that time when you were in high school?" he

asked, cupping his hands together. "And you said..." He looked at me and I looked at him, pupils dilated, the oxytocin reverberating through the interior walls of the van, the only ones in the parking lot, surrounded by miles of wilderness.

"You said that you respected Foster more than me. Kids can hurt their parents too, you know."

CHAPTER 9

What movie influenced you most in life?

I WAS TWENTY-TWO WHEN *THRIVE 1* PREMIERED. THE SANTA Cruz showing was at the Del Mar, a vintage theater with a flashing neon marquee and a line that wrapped around the corner. I wore a pressed button-up shirt, arm awkwardly slung around a girl I had recently started dating. As we shuffled closer to the concession stand, I saw the movie poster. It featured an ethnically ambiguous woman wearing a blindfold, lifting up one side with her hand, revealing a single amber eye. Across the blindfold was the tagline: *The World Is Waking Up*.

It was a sold-out show. *Thrive* spoke to the swelling movement of conspirituality, and I was surprised by how many young, attractive yoga-teacher types were in line too. The women wore flowing goddess shawls. The men dressed like Morpheus, black on black, with sacred geometry necklaces and stoic expressions—like something big was about to happen.

My date and I found seats and ate popcorn, and when the lights dimmed, I hooted and whistled. Foster entered the screen inside a CGI spaceship that was encased in a toroidal energy field, swooping through the universe from one topic to the next—free energy, gang violence, multinational banking, crop circles, vaccinations, taxation, meditation, and the depopulation agenda.

"In my research," Foster said solemnly to the camera, "I came across convincing evidence that their [the Illuminati's] plan actually includes the elimination of the majority of the global population." Arm around my date, I felt her shift in her seat. "As sick as it sounds," he continued, "it makes sense that they would be better positioned to succeed in a quest for absolute control if there are fewer of us to manage."

When my mom came on screen, wearing a lavender shirt and silver necklace, flaxen hair draped to her shoulders, I whispered as much to my date.

"It's not our fault we didn't recognize how organized and intentional this scheme is," she said, voice soft but firm. "It's our challenge."

Throughout the film, my mom and Foster evoked the flowery platitudes you'd expect in a vinyasa flow, backdropped by the beat of Big Brother at your door. Rather than cover any one topic with nuance, complexity, or intellectual honesty, they used the propaganda techniques akin to a Westboro Baptist recruitment video, cutting between gruesome close-ups of malnourished children writhing on the ground to an eagle soaring past a snow-capped mountain. The narrative is pretty hard to follow.

When the lights came up, I joined in a standing ovation, trying to ignore the obvious—my date's energy had shifted from relaxed and cuddly to a cat trapped in a box. Foster and my mom stepped on stage, their shadows cast behind them, monstrous on the now-dark screen. They took seats to field questions from the audience.

"Yeah, hi," a disgruntled man approached the microphone below the stage. He made sure to get close so his question would boom across the theater. "What do you have to say about the nine people featured in this film who have publicly denounced it?"

My mom fielded the accusation, congenial as ever. "We get slandered all the time by the mainstream media. But that's what it takes to do this work. Just last week someone from the *Santa Cruz Sentinel* came out with an article trying to debunk *Thrive*."

"Yeah," said the journalist. "I wrote the article."

My face went hot, and my date laughed nervously, her eyes darting toward the emergency exit.

In the following weeks, I learned the journalist was right. Nine of the on-camera participants had publicly denounced the film. The signatures include Deepak Chopra, Van Jones, Amy Goodwin, and Paul Hawken. Part of their letter read: "*Thrive* is a very different film from what we were led to expect when we agreed to be interviewed. We are dismayed that we were not given a chance to know its content until the time of its public release. We are equally dismayed that our participation is being used to give credibility to ideas and agendas that we see as dangerously misguided."

When *Thrive* launched, my mom predicted that free energy would be out within a year. "Once the toothpaste is out of the tube, they won't be able to put it back in!" she liked to say. I expected to see devices popping up all over the place. Perpetual-motion machines would become a multitrillion-dollar industry, and throngs of venture capitalists would deftly bring them to market. A simple demonstration on *Shark Tank* is all it would take. But the years came and went like tumbleweeds, and still, it was the same old story: Free energy exists, but the Illuminati is suppressing it.

I didn't know what to believe. I didn't even know what *she* believed. Was my mom on the vanguard? Ahead of her time? Did she know free energy was bullshit but felt a duty to support her husband—like she had in her previous marriage? Or was she part of a growing cohort of baby boomers who suffered from pathological gullibility? The world may have been waking up, but the next few years were the most confusing of my life. Friends left Santa Cruz to pursue careers. I stayed put. Like a kid who grows up in a religious household but discovers that dinosaurs are real, coming to terms with my parents' inability to parse fact from fiction didn't happen with a single "aha" moment but rather a series of staggers into adulthood.

The Thrive movement, which launched as a documentary and then spread with Facebook and newsletters, indiscriminately promoted every conspiracy theory under the sun—no matter how tenuous. The only theme was the intoxicating overconfidence that carried through the tone. That, and the color purple.

My relationship with my mom frayed, and I stopped returning her calls.

* * *

If you want to get bummed out, take a look at a Reddit forum called r/QAnonCasualties, where children connect about losing their parents to conspiracy. As I write this, it hosts nearly 300,000 children of QAnon supporters. QAnon is *Thrive* adjacent. The core of the theory revolves around the belief that a secret cabal of Satan-worshiping, child-trafficking elites controls the world, and Donald Trump is leading the fight against this dark order. The cultural movement is built on a series of cryptic posts by an anonymous user, "Q," on internet forums like 4chan and 8chan. "Q" claims to have insider knowledge of the government and military operations against this supposed deep state. I found the Reddit forum after reading an article titled, "'I Miss My Mom': Children of QAnon Believers Are Desperately Trying to De-Radicalize Their Parents." Reporter Jesselyn Cook told me that the idea for the story was first born from a QAnon rally that was happening a few blocks from her house, so she walked down the street to take a look.

"I was blown away by how many people were there. Over a thousand, for sure. And a lot of them were with their kids. It was really disturbing."

"Why was it disturbing?" I asked.

"As a child, you look to your parents to be trustworthy. They help you determine what's true. When kids are taught not to believe what they learn in textbooks, it can set them up for a tough life."

* * *

One Friday evening, when I was twenty-six, my buddy Shane came over to our surf shack—the one with the broken pilot light—and plopped down on our tattered couch. I was paying seven hundred dollars a month in rent and had no plans to leave. I was a pro surfer by then, earning just enough money to not commit myself to much at all. A toad-shaped bong sat on our TV, putrid yellowish liquid inside. Shane was a stocky artist with sad eyes and paint-splattered overalls. He listened to Alan Watts and obscure electronic music, often subjecting himself to strange health experiments: fasting, saunas, Ayurvedic herbs, breathwork, and quitting coffee, a habit that eventually led him to start MUD\WTR, the company I later wrote for.

He pulled something out of his overalls. "Dude, you gotta

listen to this," he said, giving me his phone to plug into an auxiliary cord. I turned up the volume on my living room speaker, and together, we sat for three hours and listened to an early episode of *The Joe Rogan Experience*. No matter your thoughts on Rogan, he has served as a conduit to an astonishingly diverse range of thought. From that day on, I inhaled podcasts. I discovered Tim Ferriss, Rich Roll, Neal Brennan, Brené Brown, *Tangentially Speaking,* and *Radiolab*. Sometimes, I would pull into my driveway after a day at the beach still salty and wet, and sit in my car for another twenty minutes, heater blasting, keys beeping in the ignition to keep listening.

"I want to start a podcast," I texted Shane.

The next week, he mocked up a logo for me, and I launched the show.

The premise was surf-focused. A kind of peer journalism. But I soon realized that I didn't need to limit my guests to surfers. The podcast allowed me to meet people who otherwise wouldn't make time and ask questions that might otherwise be too awkward. I interviewed a local sex educator named Amy Baldwin (Episode 23), who taught my audience of mostly dude surfers how to perform cunnilingus: "Go slower than slow, and then slower than that." Jim Fadiman (Episode 279), the father of the microdosing movement, turned out to be my neighbor and detailed the correct protocol for taking psychedelics: "Mindset, setting, and integration."

I learned powerful concepts for both interviews and life, such as mirroring. Want someone to be vulnerable? Be vulnerable yourself. Want to crank up the humor? Tell a funny story yourself. Want a guest to scratch her face? This one is freaky—scratch your own.

I studied masters like Werner Herzog. If Herzog wants someone to spill their guts, he'll simply not say anything once the person finishes their answer. The person will feel awkward and keep talking, until finally, they admit to the murder.

When steering an interview, stories are the gas, and questions are the brakes. If your guest is shy, you may need to tell a story to infuse more energy into the interview. But if the guest is on a roll, your only job is to listen, pump the brakes, and ask follow-up questions to draw out more detail.

In one of my early episodes, Shawn Dollar (Episode 5), a surfer who held the Guinness World Record for the biggest wave ever surfed, confided, for the first time publicly, that he had suffered a bad wipeout and was navigating a traumatic brain injury. Dollar had an ashy stubble and cloudy green eyes, and he wore a baseball cap low over his forehead.

"I have the same brain as a professional football player," he said. "But I'm a surfer, hitting water."

All I had to do was listen, nod, and ask the occasional follow-up question. It seemed cathartic for him to share the story, and it took balls, the kind that got him to stroke into a sixty-one-foot monster the year prior.

I remember walking away from that interview buzzing. I had stumbled upon something important.

CHAPTER 10

What's a belief that got you into trouble?

EMBOLDENED BY THE FANFARE OF *THRIVE 1*, MY MOM AND Foster made a sequel. While the first film explored the concept of free energy, the second set out to prove its existence. Most of you won't have feature-length documentaries of your parents to draw upon while gathering material for interviews. But what's your equivalent? Do you have home movies or old letters? Crawl into the attic and dig through dusty boxes like you're one of the Goonies. This is an investigative process, so investigate.

    I first watched the film at the surf shack, lying in bed with a cup of peppermint tea. I felt the warmth of the computer on my legs as the screen glowed and the film began. My mom and I had barely been speaking, and I looked forward to seeing her and Foster's faces again, if only on screen. In this sequel, Foster flew to Harare, Zimbabwe, to meet an inventor named Maxwell Chikumbutso, who claimed to have built a car, helicopter, and self-powered generator using free energy technology. The revolutionary devices apparently ran on radio frequencies drawn from the fabric of space. Foster found Maxwell on Facebook.

Neither Foster nor my mom hold degrees in physics or engineering, so on the trip to Zimbabwe, Foster brought an electrical engineer named Nils Rognerud to subdue the skeptics. On the front page of Nils's website, he introduces himself by saying, "We live in a dangerous Game of Life on this Earth, and there are established groups that do not want change. Only the real tigers survive on Earth, and even they have a hard time."

So you know he's legit.

Maxwell greeted Foster on the ground in Zimbabwe. The man was in his early forties, black, clean-shaven with an angular face, and wore a red polo shirt.

"After meeting Maxwell," Foster narrated, "I was very taken with what a gentle, true-seeming soul he seemed like." This was interesting. If Foster really had found a free energy inventor, this would be his opportunity to showcase it.

Unfortunately for Foster and the film crew, Maxwell informed him that the helicopter and the car were nonoperational, thus could not be vetted. Instead, Maxwell took Foster to his free energy generator, a perpetual-motion device he claimed could power three hundred homes. It was an impressive-looking blue box, twelve feet tall, with switches, fiber optic cables, and high-voltage stickers on the side.

"What we are looking at is called the Greener Power Off-Grid Machine," said Maxwell to the camera as he stood in front of the blue box.

"The energy frequencies that you're harnessing," Foster asked, leading the inventor to his desired answer, "are they in space all the time?"

"Yes," said Maxwell, grateful for the guidance, "but one thing that we do not know for sure is whether it is alien or man-made or from another planet or is it from God?"

Maxwell seemed unable to explain the science because, like Foster, he holds no formal education in the field. Rather, the talented storyteller crafted a narrative around himself as a tortured prodigy, charismatic enough to marshal in seed money to start a company called Saith Technologies, which *Snopes*, a reputable fact-checking website, promptly reported was oozing with Zebra shit, as their outrageous claims of perpetual-motion machines violate the Second Law of Thermodynamics.

In the next scene, Maxwell introduced Foster to his business associate, Mr. Genius, an "entrepreneur" who traded in diamonds and oil.

"Me and Maxwell will take this to another level," Mr. Genius said, gold stunner shades perched on his head as he pitched Foster on their plans to take free energy global.

"Get this," my mom cooed from her narrator's chair as she brought the audience up to speed on how Maxwell and Mr. Genius became colleagues, "they met in prison!"

I paused the film.

Something about *that* moment. *That* line. For years, I hadn't allowed myself to fully confront this part of her. This misplaced empathy. The same part of her that could look a homeless man in the eye blinded her to obvious scam artists. This is the secret con of conspiracy theories: while they preach tearing down the system, every conspiracy ends with a credit card swipe—some credulous baby boomer is always caught holding the hot potato.

When I later asked the cameraman on the trip his read on the situation, he told me, "I think Maxwell and Mr. Genius saw your mom and Foster as marks to make some extra money."

And he was right. In the following scene, Foster laid out a stack of hundred-dollar bills on his hotel room bed. After courting Foster for the first week, Maxwell suddenly became cagey, ignoring calls. "Just leave," he texted Foster. Then, just as quickly, he'd change his mind. Maybe he *would* let Foster vet the machine, for a price. Although the generator could run forever, that was the promise, it required eighteen new twelve-volt batteries to kick-start the engine. Foster would need to buy them.

But drama ensued. Foster was short on cash. Maxwell needed even *more* money to buy the batteries, and Zimbabwean banks limit withdrawals. In the next scene, they drove to Mr. Genius's nightclub to swipe Foster's credit card, and because the Zimbabwean dollar is so devalued, comically large stacks of cash piled up on Mr. Genius's office table.

When the transaction cleared, Foster thanked him for all the help.

Money secured for Maxwell to buy the new batteries, the film crew wanted to look inside the generator and record the installation—kind of an important piece of due diligence. But Maxwell became aggressive, accused Foster of bad faith, and refused. Foster acquiesced. After all, why would he have any reason not to trust these guys?

Maxwell returned to the hotel three hours later and told the crew that the new batteries had been installed. The Greener Power Off-Grid Machine was ready to be vetted.

In the final scene of the trip, night had fallen across Zimbabwe, a country where widespread corruption has collapsed the economy, resulting in a 60 percent unemployment rate and the third-lowest GDP in the world. Foster stood in front of the free energy device as streetlights illuminated a tawny hue across his face. He looked at the camera wearily, his voice thick with gravel from being strung along for more than two weeks.

"Nils will be measuring the voltage of the batteries. That will reveal whether it's what he's claimed or not."

Maxwell hooked the machine up to an arc welder. If the device could power the welder for a few hours and remain fully charged, it would prove that the energy was harmonizing with the fabric of space. Foster and Maxwell crowded around the electrical engineer. The camera zoomed in on the voltmeter.

"It's a fully charged battery!" shouted the engineer. "It's perfect."

Foster went on to say that one final battery check revealed a "shocking result." The machine had outlasted its expectancy, and the batteries were still fully charged. "This proves that the device was powered by an unknown energy source." Despite the long day, Foster smiled and put his arm around Maxwell like a brother, his eyes glistening with tears. "This is one of the happiest days of my life."

Back at the hotel, Foster called my mom. "I got your emojis!" she celebrated on speakerphone.

"The test we did today is historic," said the engineer. "I'm still digesting it because it basically means the end of fossil fuels."

The cameraman later told me, "At no point during the entire trip did we see the inside of the generator. They could have easily powered the welder with another set of batteries. I tried to tell Foster that we didn't get the footage we needed to prove anything, but he didn't want to listen."

CHAPTER 11

What is the biggest misconception about you?

"I WASN'T SURE I WANTED TO DO THIS INTERVIEW," FOSTER said as we stood in his living room, my backpack of audio gear slung over my shoulder. Outside, the free energy fountain had corroded since my last visit. "We used to hang out and get beers together, Kyle. We used to have a good relationship. But now it's so shallow." As we stood there, I felt a bead of sweat drip down my armpit. "But," he continued, "I appreciated the questions you sent, and I think more young people should interview their folks."

By the time I interviewed Foster, I had recorded over three hundred podcast episodes, and despite a tenuous relationship, I wanted to do the interview; I was ready.

Outside, an El Niño winter had descended on Santa Cruz, and the town was making national headlines. Historic storm surges combined with king tides had ripped our pier from its pilings, and debris exploded the windows of beachfront restaurants. In the living room where we stood—the place we used to do sports psychology training sessions—thick raindrops patted against the spanning windows, and beyond, mud from pregnant rivers plumed into a nickel-gray ocean.

"Well, thanks for doing it," I said, not meeting his gaze.

Foster has never been afraid of conflict. This was, in large part, what drew me to him during my teenage years. He embodied masculinity, sturdy and self-assured. Years of martial arts had taught him to speak low from his belly, and when he finished sentences, he did so with confident periods, not the nasally upward inflection so common among California surfers. Meanwhile, ET was a mild-mannered pacifist, a trickle-down quality from his own father, who was a Quaker. When I was a freshman in high school, ET had a pink-haired girlfriend who thought it would be funny to dress ET up as a collared dog for Halloween. ET just chuckled.

* * *

"Do you need to use the bathroom?" I asked as the memory vanished, and I set up the audio equipment.

"No, I'm fine," he said, studying a printed piece of paper with the questions I had emailed him. Below the questions, he had written notes to himself with a purple ink pen.

"Is your phone off?" I asked, gently closing the door.

"It is," he said. "And no one's coming up today. So we won't be distracted." If we had recorded remotely, I would have gone through the same checklist: phone off, bladder empty, doors shut. Living rooms are great for interviews because they tend to have rugs and couches to absorb echo.

"Make sure you're no more than a fist's distance away from the microphone," I said.

"Okay, first question. Will you tell me the story of ET and the purple couch?" Foster seemed surprised, then smiled. This is what I was hoping for: start the interview off on a positive note.

"Sure," he said, clearing his throat, pausing, then clearing his throat again. He does this a lot, partly due to recent health issues with his esophagus and partly because he takes his time to think through answers.

"Early into dating your mom, I was renting a house that was still unfurnished, and when I met your dad, he asked if I needed any furniture. So I said, 'Well, I actually need a couch.' I didn't expect him to have one. I mean, who keeps extra couches lying around?"

"What did ET say?"

"He asked what color I wanted."

ET drove home, climbed through his garage, and returned with a purple couch. I don't think I've ever seen my dad so proud of himself.

I took a second to reflect on my family dynamics: a biological father helping his ex-wife's new suitor move in breaks every rule in the culturally prescribed relationship book, which states that it is healthy and normal to hold lifelong resentment toward your exes and anyone who should have the audacity to fall in love with them after you.

"What is one of your proudest moments in life?" I asked. Foster looked out the window and raked his finger across his stubble.

"While at boarding school, I stood up for a guy named Dodge Dorland the third. He would walk around school in a three-piece suit, the ultimate target for bullies. One day I saw three guys from the football team heading to his dorm, planning to beat him up. I got in front of the bullies and said, 'I heard what you're going to do to my friend. That is so disgusting that you would harm another human who did nothing to you.

If you touch him, I'm gonna mess you up.' I sufficiently embarrassed them, and they backed off. That is one of my proudest moments."

Noted. Ask parents about pride; it will animate their values through a story.

"If you were to offer one piece of advice before embarking on an intimate relationship, what would you say?" I asked, genuinely curious. Like my mom, Foster signed divorce papers in a past life. He and my mom met in their fifties and are still disgustingly in love with each other. She bakes him birthday cakes with green alien candles, and he writes her love songs, strumming his guitar, dewy-eyed, with his long-ass fingernails.

"Look for virtue behind the pretty face," he said. "I used to have a teacher who would say, 'Guys! It's not the vagina. It's the virtue.' Not that the vagina isn't *great*, but it's gonna get you in a lot of trouble if you're not looking for the virtue. Aristotle said, 'Truth leads to virtue, which leads to happiness.'"

"What's the best part of your day?" I asked, moving on from the subject of vagina, virtue, and my mom.

"The best part of my day is waking up next to your mom. It connects me with the universe."

The interview was going smoothly. The tone was light, we even had banter, but midway through, I asked a question I shouldn't have: "What is the biggest misconception about you?"

"Ha," he laughed, spiking the audio waves. "The biggest misconception about me is that I'm a deluded conspiracy theorist. Fortunately, I've had several decades now to present evidence that I'm actually a conspiracy analyst. I've put my results out to the world, and it turns out that I've been accurate about virtually *everything*."

My fingernail dug into my knee, and I forced a smile.

Foster's confidence was limitless. After he released his documentaries and was promptly discredited—both by the subjects in his film and the scientific community at large—he used it as fuel for his conspiratorial fire rather than a moment to pause and reflect.

"What role has journaling played in your life?" I asked, changing the subject.

"About thirty years ago, I was involved in some advanced physics studies, and I was trying to figure out how to model all of the atoms of the periodic table in 3D, no one had ever done that, now we have computers, but back then, it was just too complicated to do in your mind, so we applied the torus to the double helix, then fractalized it into different geometries, and I hired a guy to model what the logic would reveal, and it was such a daunting task I would sit at my desk, and my brain would lock up, so I would take a break and pose the question in meditation, and suddenly, I would have visions of the answer to my questions, and there was a conversation between my rational mind and the cosmos, and we did it, we modeled the entire periodic table of elements for the first time, then I realized it was a lot bigger than the periodic table, this could work for everything, so I went back to the universe and I said 'Humanity is on the verge of destroying itself, if you give me what I need to learn what's really going on—and the way out—I will collect it, I will cohere it, and I will do everything I can to get it out to the world,' journaling is my effort to make sense of the whole."

My chest had tightened, but my smile was still on. *See the emperor, unburdened with clothes.*

Foster's dynastic advantages have afforded him the luxury of being a full-time "conspiracy analyst," buffeting himself with a small industry of grifters and sycophants, paid to confirm his ideas. He and my mom spent twenty years investing in Thrive.

It was a colossal financial failure. From 2012 to 2021, I watched them get duped into numerous scams—Zimbabwe was one of multiple.

I thought back to a moment a few years prior. Foster knew I had ditched his ideas about free energy, so he called a meeting with me in his library room. We sat around a circular table made of reclaimed wood from an old Russian freight train. The chairs were velvety purple. Since my high school years, when we did our study sessions together, the number of binders on his bookshelf had multiplied. New additions included Depopulation, Great Reset, and Mind Control. Years of resentment had compounded. I hated that I ever believed his goofy conspiracy theories, defended him when people said he was nuts, ignored his logical jumps as he bounced from one to the next like we were living in a fucking fun house. And I hated that he enlisted my mom. His ideas never would have made it off the block without her. Sitting with him in the library room, I didn't pull punches.

"You are financially insulated from reality," I said coldly.

"It's probably best that you stop looking into what's really going on," he retorted. "It could be bad for your career and your psyche. It's like telling a kid that Santa Claus isn't real before they're ready."

At the end of the meeting, we agreed not to talk about his conspiracies unless I explicitly brought it up. This felt like a healthy boundary, but another aspect of our relationship fell away: laughter.

I thanked Foster for the time, packed up my audio equipment, and drove away. I'd like to say that the interview brought us closer together, but I'm not sure it did. I was too angry to listen openly. For the rest of the day, I felt vaguely sad, like when you reconnect with a childhood friend, only to realize you no longer share much in common. When interviewing your parents, it's easy to let expectations creep in. You may hope it will heal your wound. But it may not.

CHAPTER 12

What trip will you always remember?

I MOVED OUT OF THE SURF SHACK, SOLD MOST OF MY SHIT, and downsized my 1997 Ford RV, Starflyte. I took the podcast on the road. It was the first time I had moved away from Santa Cruz. Along the way, I learned the skills that would prepare me to sit down with Foster again. One of my extended trips was to Montana, a state with an average of seven people per square mile, and clear night air is cut by the bugle of bull elk, deep within the tremendous wild.

"Go back to California!"

These were my welcome words as I drove Starflyte through downtown Bozeman on a windless summer day. The words came out unrushed, vowels flat, with a hint of drawl. I spotted my greeter in the rearview mirror. The man rode away on a rusty bicycle, his fubsy belly jiggling along the bumpy road.

Bozeman is a mirror image of Santa Cruz. Locals love their nature almost as much as they hate outsiders. The city is cupped by craggy peaks on all sides, and the Gallatin River runs north from Yellowstone National Park.

Early into my expedition, I found Stacey's Old Faithful Bar & Steakhouse, a cowboy bar established in 1963 with the slogan, "Where the West is still the West." Black-and-white rodeo photos covered the walls, and ambient chatter was broken only by the crack of pool balls and, occasionally, a human skull. The first time I walked into Stacey's, I scanned the room, looked down at my retro purple sweater, did a 180, and returned with my camo jacket. Only months later did I learn that wearing camouflage inside a bar is like wearing a wetsuit inside a grocery store. The mark of a poser.

"Where you from?" a grizzled old rancher asked from a nearby barstool. The man resembled the last surviving member of the Lewis and Clark expedition.

"Santa Cruz," I said, careful not to include my home state. Perhaps he would think I was visiting from Santa Cruz, Bolivia, or Santa Cruz, Philippines. After we exhausted the topic of weather in Montana, a mercurial beast that changes moods every ten minutes, he asked what I did for work.

"Um, I'm a pro surfer." Technically, this was still true. But the title was starting to feel awkward, like a fully grown adult who still sports Velcro light-up shoes.

The old-timer laughed. "Not *another* pro surfer in Montana."

Beyond Stacey's are ranches—millions of acres of ranches—home to cows with muscular frames, long lashes, and bored eyes. Aside from the odd chat at Stacey's, I was mostly alone. I would park Starflyte by a pasture outside of town, set up a camp chair, eat Amy's Kitchen canned lentil soup, and stare at cows. Sometimes these laconic creatures would approach the fence, chew cud, and stare back at me, neither of us with anything better to do.

It was nice, for a few days.

Van life promised freedom, but it felt closer to solitary confinement on wheels. Novelty faded to boredom, then loneliness, then existential crisis. I was, after all, living in a car. I had recently gone through a painful breakup, was barely speaking to my mom, and didn't have a friend for a thousand miles. My career as a writer was rudderless, and my self-esteem was sinking fast. Put anyone in a metal box for eighteen hours a day, and their thoughts will turn on them. Some days, I would be taken by waves of paranoia, grandiosity, and depression, all in the span of an hour. When you live outside of society, it's easy to think of yourself as superior. You drive against the blinding lights of evening traffic and see humans shackled to their nine-to-fives. You know something they don't, and you're right—but what you forget is that they know something you don't, too.

Luckily, I never went full cowbell in Montana. The first few weeks were hard, but eventually something shifted and alone time led to quietude. Before I left Santa Cruz, my life was a frenetic hum of context shifting. Friends dropped by the surf shack at random and my phone was never more than two feet away. This lack of focus has caused much of my twenties to blur. I know I was doing *something* during those years, but what? Answers can be found in my social media feed. An archaeological dig of wasted time. When I started my podcast, I was forced to acknowledge that my attention span sucked.

If a guest told a dull story, my eyes glazed, and I would drift into a galaxy far away. It was like that scene from *The Simpsons* when Marge goes, "Homer, are you even listening?" and the camera zooms into Homer's brain to show a monkey playing the tambourine.

Starflyte became my rehab center for digital addiction. I bought a clear, cylindrical cookie jar with a lock and digital timer. I would quarantine my phone in the jar, set the timer for five hours, then hike the trails, trudging through thick groves of lodgepole pine, pink bitterroot flowers, and moss-covered granite, equipped with water, a turkey sandwich, and bear spray, all the while thinking, "How incredibly stupid of me not to bring my phone." And as the first signs of light spilled into the valley each morning, I would sprint out of Starflyte in board shorts, down a trail cut through tall brown grasses, cold prickling my feet, goose bumps along my forearms, wade into the Gallatin, take three deep breaths, grab a cobblestone rock, and let the current sweep my legs.

* * *

Montana wasn't all reverie and solitude. Once I got my bearings, I started recording podcasts, averaging two a week. One interview was with legendary travel writer and co-founder of *Outside Magazine*, Tim Cahill (Episode 362)—whose podcast was filled with subtle journalism advice. Cahill was blithe, in his late seventies, wearing a stained blue shirt, spectacles, and a baseball cap.

"You're a travel writer," he said. "You've got twenty minutes. Sit down and observe a single object—a statue, for instance—and write about it. First, you'll see a gray statue with a guy on a horse. But if you hold focus long enough, you will form an opinion about it. You may think, 'That is a very bullying statue. I don't like the guy, I don't like the artist, I don't like that it's there! And look at these buildings around it. They're falling apart.' Start with something specific, spend time with it, and layers of detail will appear."

I later considered the statue as a child's perception of his or her parents. How many of us see parents as relics? Solitary, unmoving, boring at first glance. Only when we hold focus can we see their cracks and folds and textures. Spend enough time with a statue, and it almost starts to move.

* * *

I met another friend named Kevin Grunewald. He was a hunter in his early thirties, athletic, with a clean-trimmed ginger beard and corded forearms. Originally from Wisconsin, Kevin was a human iceberg who kept most of himself to himself. Only over the course of a year did I learn that he had trapped bats in the Australian outback, guided clients through bear country in Alaska, and dissected zebrafish embryos in a university laboratory in Wisconsin.

"The human brain adapts to its surroundings," he said (Episode 338). "Our values are shaped by landscapes."

Because of this insight, Kevin traded microscopes for binoculars and now works as a guide in Yellowstone National Park, where he hosts tours to rainbow-colored geysers and three-hundred-foot cascading waterfalls. "They say that you're an average of the five people you associate with most," he said. "Three of my people are a dog, a bear, and a fish."

Kevin was also one of the few people I met who had interviewed his dad. I asked what he had hoped to get out of it.

"I wanted to learn about my dad in different periods of his life and understand his decision-making process when he was my age."

"Do you remember any questions you asked?"

"I asked about his first successful deer hunt."

Kevin's dad gave him a rifle at twelve. Hunting was how they built memories. His family had a cabin in Wisconsin, where he learned to hunt whitetail deer and fish for bass, walleye, northern pike, and panfish. The cabin had a stone fireplace, and at night, Kevin and his dad would stare into the flame, only the crack of a log to break the silence.

"We spent a lot of nonverbal time together," he said. "The interview gave me a chance to ask pointed questions."

Now that Kevin lives in Montana, he and his dad don't talk as much as they used to. When they finished the interview, his dad thanked him and suggested they plan another hunt soon.

"Anything you would've done differently?" I asked.

"Yeah, if you do the interview remotely, pay for the Zoom Pro account. It tried to kick me off after thirty minutes. Oh, and don't stop recording, the best shit they say is going to be after the interview is over."

I left Montana in autumn. The nights closed in faster, ice gripped my windows, and aspens flickered gold. As I crossed a state line, I passed one final ranch with worn wooden fences and cows who stared. I thought of something Kevin had told me: The Latin root for *ruminate* is *ruminare*, which means to *chew over again*. It refers to the first stomach compartment of ruminant animals—cattle, sheep, bison—where cud is regurgitated and chewed a second time during digestion.

When I got to Montana, I liked to imagine that Starflyte was my spaceship. But when I left, I realized that the correct metaphor for Starflyte was not a spaceship but the first stomach of a cow. During that trip, I learned to meditate, journal, and keep my phone locked in a cookie jar. I learned to deal with discomfort, essential skills for interviewers. Your parents may not be charismatic storytellers. They may speak slowly or lose their train of thought. Be patient. As I passed the ranch on my way out of Montana, it occurred to me that I had gotten it all wrong: Cows aren't bored; they're just thinking it through.

CHAPTER 13

How do you manage stress?

"I THINK I'M HERE." I TEXTED AT 3:01 P.M. ON A THURSDAY in Ojai, California, pulling up to the house in Starflyte. The band Galactic blared from my tape player and smoke billowed from the tailpipe, blanketing the garden out front of the quaint little house, which had succulents, native pollinators, and a rain catchment system.

"I'm ready," a blue text promptly swooshed back.

Katie Hendricks, PhD, (Episode 328) walked out her front door wearing a floral shirt and blue jeans. She was in her seventies, with trimmed gray hair and a giving smile. Twenty years ago, Katie and her husband, Gay, moved to Ojai. The coauthor couple wrote more than forty books, trained thousands of coaches, appeared on *Oprah*, and hosted seminars around the globe. As a lifelong dancer and transpersonal psychologist, Hendricks teaches how emotional stress ripples through the body: tight shoulders, shallow breathing, aching lower back—we all have our favorite flavor of stress. I wanted to talk to Hendricks because these physical stressors can show up when interviewing your parents. How do you let them go? What do you do if, midway through the interview, your mom touches a wound, crumbling your emotional floorboards? Aside from firing back with your own vicious zinger, I was all out of advice.

"Gay snapped his femur in five places," Hendricks said almost cheerfully as she led me through the house. Two ashen cats meowed as we walked into her cool, carpeted office. Hendricks sat on the couch, and behind her hung a watercolor painting of the Topatopa mountain range. She propped the microphone on a pillow in her lap and held it with the confidence of someone who had done this before.

"I've heard you say that appreciation has the highest ROI of any relationship move. Why is that?" I asked.

"The biggest killer for relationships, not just romantic, but parent–child relationships too, is blame and criticism. It's the most common interaction. I remember my mom saying, 'Katie, I'm just telling you this for your own good.' And even as she said it, I could feel myself withdraw. But appreciation is genuine contact. You're offering sensitive attention, and you're noticing what's working rather than what's not working."

"Can you give an example?" I asked.

"Well," she pondered, searching the room. "I see that you brought your whole podcast setup in a backpack." She gestured to my tattered backpack, which sat in the corner. "I appreciate how compact it is. That's not profound, but it's accurate. I'm giving you my attention and noticing something specific. Your emotional brain will register that."

"What if the interview starts to go off the rails?" I asked.

"In conversation, hardly anyone takes time to pause," Katie said. "But pausing allows things to settle."

I've observed this in my podcasts. Although regular conversations and interviews can sound alike, there are a few key differences. Let's say your dad launches into politics, you can simply wait until he's finished—pause, pause—then ask a different question. Katie told me that pausing also applies to your body. If you notice your shoulders tense, take a few deep breaths through your nose, even stop the interview, and pick back up after a breather. Literally, shake it off. (Just say you need to pee.)

She also underscored the power of humor during difficult exchanges. "One thing that tends to drop off in drama is your sense of humor. I love Robin Williams and George Carlin because their comedy is about stepping into a lighter reality that you create."

In the 1970s, psychologists John Gottman and Robert Levenson learned to predict if a married couple was headed for divorce with 90 percent accuracy. They put couples in a room and asked them to solve a conflict over the course of fifteen minutes. If the couple had five positive exchanges for every one negative exchange, they would reliably stay together. Some of the key examples of positive exchange were appreciation, affection, and jokes. It's known today as the Gottman Ratio.

During our podcast, Hendricks told me that one year she was home for the holidays, cooking dinner with her mother. She had been exploring prenatal psychology and asked about her birth—where they were living, what life was like—and her mother just blurted it out. "You know, we never wanted you."

"You'd think I would have been devastated," Hendricks said. "But when I had the truth confirmed, I could stop looking for something that wasn't there."

Her mother was an artist who raised Katie with a sense of refinement and color that she holds to this day. Once she knew the truth, she was able to appreciate the connection. They spent more time going to museums and bonding through art.

"For people who suspect that their parents didn't want them, do you recommend approaching this in an interview?" I asked.

"That's a separate conversation," she said. "Ideally, with a therapist in the room. Families are the Olympics of communication. The interview is to establish a connection, approach with appreciation, and experience your parents as evolving works of art, not your own personal improvement projects."

CHAPTER 14

Describe the culture around you when you were in college. How did it influence your outlook on the world?

I WALKED INTO THE FIRST INTERVIEW WITH MY MOM KEEPing Katie's advice in mind. The sky was gunmetal gray and water dripped from her bird feeders with rhythmic tempo. I set our microphones on the circular mahogany table next to a cup of lemon water. She wore a gray sweater with a mountain lion stencil, black joggers, and running shoes. I saw her age when she leaned into the microphone, clasping her hands on the table, thin as binder paper, tangled with varicose veins.

In 1968, my mom packed her car and drove north to Berkeley to begin her first year of college during a time in American history when tear gas was as common as Bay Area fog.

JFK had been shot in Dallas. LBJ would draft two million young men to Vietnam to fight in a sweltering war that dragged out for nineteen years. One hundred thousand hippies trundled

Volkswagen vans to Golden Gate Park for the Summer of Love. Thanks to Ken Kesey and his Merry Pranksters, more young Americans took acid in a single year than they had in all the prior years combined.

When interviewing your parents, it may be helpful to linger on their twenties. These are formative years when we are out of the house and thrust into culture. We learn drinking habits and thinking habits that can set the trajectory for the rest of our lives. As Meg Jay wrote in her book *The Defining Decade*, "Personality can change more during our twenties than at any other decade in life... As we age, we feel less like leaves and more like trees."

"Why did you choose to go to Berkeley for college?" I asked.

"Berkeley was the only place I wanted to go," she said. "Everything was about freedom. I lived in a house with four other people, and we changed rooms every month, just for the hell of it."

"Can you tell me about your class with Carl Sagan?" Narrowing my question to draw out details.

The famous astronomer blasted a message into the asteroid belt, hoping aliens might respond. The *Pioneer* plaque was a physical message made of metal, the heart of which is a constellation of lines and dashes—a cosmic address for our pale blue dot. Beside the lines stand two naked humans: man and woman. The man with his hand raised, a universal hello...or "Don't come closer, I'm naked!" depending on how you look at it.

"Sagan bounced into the room," she said. "During one class, there had been some discovery, and he was dumbfounded that it wasn't headline news. 'Can you believe it?' he shouted at the auditorium. 'These journalists wouldn't know an important story if it smacked them in the face!' He made us believe that the world was new, discoveries could still be made."

The Bay Area was the epicenter of a cultural revolution that hadn't happened before or since, and Hunter S. Thompson's quote summed it up: "[There was] a fantastic universal sense that whatever we were doing was right, that we were winning... There was no point in fighting—on our side or theirs. We had all the momentum; we were riding the crest of a high and beautiful wave."

My mom wove a lot of sixties ideology into my homeschool curriculum. Despite the more eccentric topics—free energy and the Illuminati—others were planted firmly on the ground. My favorites were her lessons in environmental activism, a movement that bloomed in the sixties. Because I refused to sit still, my mom would edify on the move. We would walk together through Lighthouse Field, a nature preserve with dirt paths, eucalyptus trees, and monarch butterflies that made their autumn pit stop in Santa Cruz, before migrating north to British Columbia in spring. On one of those walks, she told me about *The Whole Earth Catalog*, a five-dollar magazine distributed to millions of Americans between 1968 and 1971. It was a catalog of alternative thought and a protest against blind consumerism, luxurious living, war, environmental destruction, and the white-picket-fence American Dream. Like a porno mag, a young hippie might hide the catalog from their parents, then flaunt it to friends.

"Do you see many parallels between the sixties movement and today?" I asked. This was a preplanned question. As I had journaled interview ideas, I noticed how much of the conspirituality movement referenced and remixed ideas from the 1960s. The psychedelic renaissance, transpersonal psychology, and Eastern spirituality were all coming back into vogue.

"It was so different," she countered. "Today there's a movement to make people who question authority feel isolated." Her blue eyes caught mine. "When I see Berkeley students shut down controversial speakers, I think, *That never would have happened in my day*. We trained ourselves to listen to people we disagreed with."

I nodded.

"How did it feel to be at Berkeley during the Vietnam War?" I asked. As Charles Duhigg recommended, I didn't ask about the facts of war, I asked how she felt about it.

"It was terrifying," she said. "The war backdropped everything. We would gather at a friend's house off Telegraph Avenue and watch the draft on TV. The announcer would reach into a bin and pull out little blue capsules." The capsules resembled flu pills, each with a small, rolled paper inside. The announcer would unfurl the paper and call out a birthday. If a young man's birthday was called, he went to war.

"It was like bingo," she said.

One night, she watched the draft with two brothers, and one of their birthdays was announced on TV.

"Richie became a medic on the front lines," she said. "When he came home, he could only sleep with the lights on. He became quiet. But not a peaceful quiet, you know."

Her story made me think of a trip I once took to Washington, DC. On a warm spring day with cherry trees in bloom, I rode a rental bike to the historical monuments and museums—Lincoln Memorial, the Smithsonian, the White House. I stopped by the Newseum, a museum dedicated to the history of journalism. I walked to a gallery of the Vietnam War and was confronted by a Pulitzer Prize–winning photograph of a young girl fleeing her village, her naked body scorched by napalm. The photograph was taken on June 8, 1972. My mom had just graduated college.

The media landscape was scaling up on broadcast networks, and young baby boomers like my mom, the largest generation in history to that point, watched in horror as WAR was delivered in explosive color for the first time ever. My mom became an anti-war protestor, marching through the streets of San Francisco, surrounded by the clanking bells of trolley cars and the saltwater mist of Ocean Beach sailing toward the picketing streets.

"A lot of it was ill-conceived," she reflected. "I remember blocking traffic on Golden Gate Bridge, just making it a hassle for anyone who had to get anywhere."

Governor Ronald Reagan called Berkeley "a haven for communist sympathizers, protesters, and sex deviants." He vowed to crack down.

People's Park in Berkeley was a hub of countless walkouts, sit-ins, and candlelight vigils. On a day that became known as Bloody Thursday, May 15, 1969, my mom marched with six thousand protestors down Telegraph Avenue. Reagan sent troops in riot gear. Protestors set a patrol car on fire. Helicopters glazed the neighborhood with tear gas. Initial attempts by the police to disperse the protesters were unsuccessful, and more officers swarmed in from surrounding cities. One hundred twenty-eight Berkeley residents were admitted to local hospitals for head trauma, shotgun wounds, and other serious injuries inflicted by police. A young man was shot and died, and another was blinded after taking buckshot to the face.

"It turned out that Reagan infiltrated the marches," she said. "Agents disguised themselves as protestors and started fights to turn the demonstrations violent." This checked out. The FBI had launched a covert operation called COINTELPRO aimed at surveilling and discrediting activist groups that the government viewed as subversive.

As she told me about the Vietnam War protests, it made me wonder if, in some strange, circuitous way, the sixties movement was the ember that sparked the conspiratorial ideology among baby boomers. The prism you use to view the world in your twenties can become the way you see things for the rest of your life. How many former anti-war protesters now found homes in conspiracy chat rooms? Both movements were born from a belief in individual expression above all else. The famous sixties slogan "If It Feels Good, Do It," depicting a bear scratching its back against a tree, was a rallying cry to do your own thing—innocuous at a glance, but perhaps it led to a psychology that the government was the problem. Over time, the hippies slowly slid right, protests moved online, and tear gas morphed into chemtrails.

"If you want to understand the sixties, you need to understand the war," my mom finished.

As our first of three interviews came to a close, I took her point one step further: The more I began to understand the sixties, the more I began to understand her.

CHAPTER 15

What's a memory that makes you cringe with embarrassment?

WHEN I WAS IN JUNIOR HIGH, MY FRIENDS AND I WERE SURF-ing on the edge of a reef shelf at the base of a cliff, overlooked by a nunnery. The swells ricocheted off an exposed wall of reef, doubled back, and a surfer could ride the white water into a larger oncoming wave, creating a wedge straight into the tube.

The wave thundered down the reef, throaty and mean. I paddled hard, stood up, and flawlessly bottom turned, weaving through the inside of a barrel that could have engulfed an F-350 utility truck. When I shot out the end, I stood tall, fists over my head.

One of my friends had recently been involved in a skateboarding accident—a broken arm, or minor head injury, I can't remember exactly—and he was filming with a Hi8 camera down the beach. I belly rode the next wave to shore, scurried up the sand, saltwater dripping from my nose, and asked if he filmed my wave. He mumbled that he wasn't sure, peering through the viewfinder as he filmed the next passing surfer.

That night, while having dinner with ET, our phone rang. These were the days before cell phones, and ET answered.

"It's for you," he said.

"Thiermann!" My friend huffed through the other end of the corded phone. "We filmed your wave. You've gotta see it."

It was a school night, but I forced ET to drive me to my friend's house and wait outside while I reviewed my heroic ride. When I walked into the room, five friends sat around the television, Hi8 camera plugged in, an image of a wave frozen on screen.

"Play it," one said.

The clip that followed showed a towheaded boy drop into an unremarkable wave, bottom turn, and, in what appeared to be an attempt to wash shampoo out of his eyes using a poorly functioning showerhead, gets hit squarely in the face by the lip.

Then the boy thrusts his arms in triumph for no apparent reason and kicks out of the wave.

The room erupted in laughter.

First, I feigned mistaken identity, claiming it was another blond boy with green skulls stenciled on his surfboard. But after they replayed the clip half a dozen times, each rewind of the tape mocking me with the sound of its high-pitched squeal, the truth hit me: I was a kook.

On the drive home, I told ET it was a great wave.

* * *

When we interview our parents, they are recalling stories from memory, and memory stinks. Had it not been for the damning video evidence, I could have gone my entire life woefully mistaken about my not-so-epic ride.

I wanted to get a better handle on how memory works, so I reached out to David Shenk, author of *The Forgetting*, a book about Alzheimer's. Shenk said that when you think of a memory, your brain doesn't summon the original event. Rather, you remember the last time you told the story. It's a game of telephone with yourself. Over time you might add little details or omit others to make the story juicier. This process can be entirely unconscious.

"Memory is like a gravel path," said Shenk. "When a memory arrives, you sprinkle a few pebbles on the path. Each time you think of the memory, you sprinkle a few more. If you tell a story a thousand times, nine hundred and ninety-nine are going to be the memory of the memory."

Although our brains can slow as we age, one area where evolution shows mercy to the elderly is in their bias to remember the good times better than the bad.

In a story in *Psychology Today*, two groups of people, young and old, were hooked up to brain scanners and shown a series of photographs meant to evoke both positive and negative emotions. When it came to the older cohort, the amygdala—a part of your brain responsible for emotional behavior—was activated equally by positive and negative images. Younger adult brains, on the other hand, were activated more by negative images. Afterward, the two cohorts were asked to recall as many images as they could, and the old folks recalled significantly more positive images than negative ones. The study's lead researcher, Susan Turk Charles, PhD, said the findings support the Socio-Emotional Selectivity Theory: As we become more aware of our limited time on earth, we direct our attention to positive thoughts and memories. "It's not because negative things don't happen to older adults. It's that they're not dwelling on them."

While I was on a call with David Shenk, he recounted a story from third grade. He was a puny little guy, and one day on the dodgeball court, the biggest bully in school, an ogre named Peter, spotted little David quivering on the edge of the court. The bully smirked, wound up, then fired the red ball. The ball whizzed through the air, as it zeroed in on its target: David's nose. There was no time to think, so he raised his hands to protect his face from maximal impact. A hush fell upon the schoolyard, he looked down, and the red ball was in his hands. He stared at it, stunned. The bully was out. David beat Goliath.

More than forty years later, Shenk told the story over a Zoom call in vivid detail, holding his hands up to the screen like a catcher's mitt as he acted out the final crescendo.

"I've told that story so many times you'd literally have to cut it out of my brain," he said. The underdog who acted courageously is a helpful concept for him to embody. It provides evidence that he can act under pressure.

When interviewing your parents, the truth of their stories is secondary to how the stories help them assemble their self-identities. Do they play the hero? The victim? Do they have a sense of humor about themselves? Thinking about their stories through this lens is more important than finding the capital-T Truth. That's what I believe, anyway.

"Come to think of it," said Shenk, "I remember the bully throwing that dodgeball when I was in *third* grade, but I don't even think I met that guy until I was in *sixth* grade."

CHAPTER 16

Which sibling are you closest with?

MY FAVORITE WRITER, DAVID SEDARIS, WAS ONCE ASKED BY a fan how he developed such a close relationship with his sister Amy. "I have kids," the fan said, "and I want them to have a strong bond. What do you recommend I do?"

Sedaris responded, "Become an alcoholic."

No matter your childhood, siblings can help you with the interview process. This is a journalistic endeavor, and siblings are valuable sources. They go through the same major events as you, but they do so from a different vantage point. As you prepare for the interviews, it may be worth talking to your siblings first. Run through your interview with them, and see what questions they might add. Even if you don't take their advice, it will pressure test your approach. Siblings can also be good resources to help fill in your own childhood gaps. They can set the record straight. Because siblings are very honest.

I'm the youngest of five. My mom and dad had a boy and a girl apiece before they hitched up and had me. If that last sentence confused you, don't worry; you need a Venn diagram to map my family. Toby is the closest to me in terms of age. He's my half brother and seven years my senior. Different moms, same dad.

To give you a sense of the influence Toby had on my life, bear with me as we take a quick aside to Burning Man—the most annoyingly talked-about festival on earth.

I was fifteen the first time I went. The promise of a mass topless bike ride called Critical Tits was all the convincing I needed to venture out to a dry lake bed four hundred miles from the nearest ocean. ET thought it would be good for me. He wanted me to see creativity for the sake of creativity. I wanted to see tits for the sake of tits.

ET drove Toby and me to Burning Man in a Dodge RV that he had picked up for $1,000. That night, we made it to Reno and camped in a Walmart parking lot. As the sun crested over Gerlach the next morning, the last town before Burning Man, buildings vanished, mountains shrank away, and when we took a hard right off the highway to the entrance lane, all that remained was a desert lake bed, flat as the ocean on an August day.

The line was hours long, and as we inched forward, a mild dust storm kicked up, shrouding the scene in a dramatic, slow-motion feel. Hours later, the three of us reached the gate.

"Any virgins here?" a heavyset man with a peacock thong and top hat asked as we reached the entrance gate.

I raised my hand. Then realized the question wasn't literal.

"Get out here!" he commanded, thrusting a baton in my hand. I rolled in the alkaline dust, clanked a bell, and through dry, cracked windpipes, shouted, "I'm not a virgin anymore!" Cars honked in celebration.

"Welcome home," Peacock Man said, squeezing me into his hairy chest.

Toby was twenty-two and home from college, meaning, of course, that he had the world *entirely* figured out. Whatever my brother told me, I took as gospel. (When I was five, he made me believe that humans had a limited number of times they could blink in their lifetime before they went blind.)

I talked like him, skateboarded like him, and dressed like him.

Toby hoisted two storage boxes of costumes out of the RV and threw me hand-me-downs to wear for the week: a cowboy hat, kimono, and lime green tae kwon do shorts. He snapped on tights and a tutu, we saddled into our cruiser bikes, and we set off for the day. As we rode our bikes to the center of the playa, waves of heat warping the lake bed, I craned my head at the Man, a goliath wooden structure fifty feet tall, the most impressive piece of art I had ever seen. I waited for Toby's reaction.

"So cool," he said.

"Totally."

And so it went. I drafted off Toby for the week, mirroring his responses. We hung off geodesic domes and danced until our socks were red with blood blisters. On the night of the burn, the three of us—ET, Toby, and I—huddled on the cracked lake bed floor and watched flames lick the Nevada sky as heat beat against my face. Sixty thousand people in celebration.

"So cool," whispered Toby.

"Totally."

* * *

As I prepared for my second interview with ET—the first was two years prior on my podcast—I visited Toby at his house, where he lives with his wife, three-year-old daughter, and housemates.

It was nighttime, and Toby slid off the cover of his secondhand Jacuzzi, which he proudly bought for one-eighth the asking price on Craigslist. The lights were dim, and my skin prickled with goose bumps, a low hum of bubbles between us. I set my phone on the edge of the tub and recorded the conversation using my Voice Memos app. Toby has ET's eyes and floppy brown hair that curls down his forehead in the shape of a heart. He is sensitive but taciturn. Not one to talk about the ol' feelings unprompted. Because of this, I angled myself diagonally to him, on the other side of the tub. Vulnerable talks between men go better when not face-to-face. We feel less threatened. This is why dudes only open up to each other in car rides.

"Where do you think Dad's love for the Flea comes from?" I asked. Toby's garage is filled with the same voluminous array of secondhand trinkets. The only difference between him and ET is that Toby keeps his stuff labeled in boxes, whereas ET needs only a general mind map of everything he owns. Nothing brings Toby more joy than sniffing out a deal, a proclivity he adopted early, riding his tricycle around the Flea with our dad.

"It's treasure hunting!" Toby said—verbatim to ET's description. "Dad loves it when someone calls him in a pinch. It's like, one of his favorite fucking things. He'll show up so fast with the exact thing they need."

I thought about Foster and the purple couch.

"Part of it might go back to the Great Depression," he continued, arms resting on the back of the tub. "When ET was a kid, he got five bucks to live for the entire month—food, clothes, entertainment. Now when he sees a deal, he can't pass it up. Honestly, I feel like I adopted it too. Three generations past the Depression, and I'm still fucking collecting shit." Toby paused. "But I'm not a hoarder. I just have an affinity for good stuff."

"What would you ask ET about if you interviewed him?"

"ET doesn't treat a billionaire like a billionaire or a teenager like a teenager. I'd ask him where that skill came from. I've never been afraid to leave ET alone with my friends. Most people wouldn't leave their dad around friends. They'd be afraid he'd say something fucking weird. Over the years, it's insane how many friends have pulled me aside and been like, 'You have a really cool dad.'"

"Did ET get you into filmmaking?" I asked. Chlorine fizzed into my nostrils as I slunk down into the Jacuzzi.

"In some ways." He paused. "But he's always been...competitive with me. You know that. He has this inability to be like, 'Wow, you did a great job.'"

Toby absently splashed water with the back of his hand, and a small wave rippled across the tub into darkness.

"I wish he could see me as an extension of his creative lineage. You know, like, if I go on to do great things, he had something to do with that."

Toby became a filmmaker after college. He started his own production company and moved into the same building as ET, one floor below. If my brother ever walked upstairs to share his work, ET would respond, "Good job." Incapable of stopping there, he'd add, "But if you did this one thing differently, it would've been a lot better."

"Where do you think that competitiveness comes from?" I asked.

"I think he didn't fully achieve his dreams in feature films or whatever, but I've seen firsthand what it's like to work on Hollywood sets. It fucking sucks. The amount of life you have to give up to be able to chase that dream is insane. ET's done a bunch of super cool shit and paved his own way straight out of college. If he felt proud of himself, maybe he could feel proud of me."

There was a schism in the way ET talked *about* Toby versus how he talked *to* Toby.

ET loved to tell the story of the year he and Toby were hired to film Burning Man. They drove out together and set up a forty-foot crane called a Jimmy Jib to capture art installations. Midway through a shot, a ranger warned that a dust storm was careening across the desert with sixty-mile-an-hour winds.

"It takes an hour to deconstruct a crane," said ET. "Your brother and I did it in twenty minutes, then hunkered down in the van right as the storm hit. The windshield was coffee-colored, I'm telling you, and people started banging on the side of the van to take shelter. Toby slid the door open and made margaritas for everyone in the back of the van. Toby's a problem solver. I like problem solvers. He has this amazing ability to make everyone he meets feel included."

Toby would never hear this version.

"Why do you think he's not competitive with me?" I had never asked Toby this before.

"Because you wrote him off," he said, rubbing his eyes. "It all started with that math test."

I stared blankly.

"You don't remember that?"

The memory rushed in all at once. Sophomore year at public school. Algebra 2 finals. A friend took the test the week before and gave me the answers. On the day of the test, I sat at my desk with a hidden piece of paper containing his notes. I was a nervous wreck, and as I filled in my test, a tingle of adrenaline crawled up my cheeks like a vine.

The next day, as I walked into math class, my teacher stopped me. "Kyle, please see me after class." I remember the dull thud in my temples as the words left my teacher's mouth, as if in slow motion. The bell rang, and he handed me a slip to go to the principal's office. I gathered my stuff and walked down the crowded halls. My depth perception blurred, and I gripped the straps of my backpack like it was a parachute pack, hoping to find the nearest cliff to hurl myself off. I vowed that no matter the threats, I wouldn't cave. Unfortunately for my test dealer, he had also shared his answers with a rat named Renée. As I took a final breath and readied myself to knock on the door to the principal's office, it swung open, and Renée spilled out, raining mascara.

It turned out that our teacher had switched the tests from one week to the next, so I got all the right answers to all the wrong questions. I was fucked. The 0 percent score brought my class grade down to a D. The following year, I would be forced to retake Algebra 2. It seems silly now, but at fifteen, this was devastating—I was dumb, a dunce, a loser who flunked classes.

"You were super embarrassed about it," said Toby. "And your mom swooped in with the homeschool option. ET didn't think homeschooling was a smart move, so you told him to fuck off, and I think he's had to tread lightly because you just…"

"Told him to fuck off."

"Yeah, you blew him off, you know."

I sat on the edge of the Jacuzzi as waves of heat shunted off me. I felt the same embarrassment from high school, only this time for how I had treated my dad.

"Then you adopted all the conspiracy shit hook, line, and sinker. A public school. A public university. Those systems can force you to…"

"Grow up," I finished for him.

"Yeah, I was worried about you. Your mom is super smart, but she coddled the shit out of you. I thought you were gonna spend the rest of your life surfing Steamer Lane and working at a fucking burger spot."

A missing piece of the story with my mom clicked into place. That math test was the last real one I ever took, the last scholastic reality I ever bumped up against. The memory was clear in my mind and aching in my stomach. Throughout my childhood, I saw myself as smart, and the test took a sledgehammer to that fragile identity. Conspiracy theories were the solution. Free energy was the solution. If I didn't grasp a concept, I could roll my eyes and say that the whole system was rigged. When I finally lost faith in my mom and Foster's logic, I lost that intoxicating sense of confidence.

"That test," Toby said. "That was the moment, a thousand percent. I can't believe you blocked that out."

CHAPTER 17

What should you apologize for?

SOME OF YOU ARE WAITING ON AN APOLOGY FROM YOUR parents. Every year at Thanksgiving, a small part of you hopes they'll take you aside, atone for their blunders, and skillfully deliver a paragraph-long apology, preferably over a cup of chamomile tea. If this is you, don't hold your breath. Remember, our parents grew up in the days when you could play with mercury in the dentist's office, preceded mostly by wagons and illiterate farmers. Talking about our feelings, let alone apologizing, is a fairly new advent in human history. And let's be honest—you were a petulant little shit. There are probably a few things you regret saying, spray-painting, or stealing, and if it feels within the bounds of reason, offering your own apology can do wonders to air out a relationship and make an interview go more smoothly.

The day after I talked to Toby, I drove to ET's house. It was time for our second interview. We had recorded the first more than two years ago during the podcast that kicked this project off. As I walked through the front door, I was met by the ethereal sound of Enya—ET's celebrity crush—and the smell of salmon wafted from the kitchen. My dad's house is an artistic vortex. Cluttered, cultured, and odd. Like him. Volumes of Shakespeare and poetry were perched on his shelves, as was a pine cone, seashells, an owl wing, and a haunting Huichol Indian mask that he picked up from the Flea.

"Hey, Mr. Dude," he called from the kitchen, apron on, spatula in hand. On the wall beside him hung the iconic framed photo of Steven Spielberg's movie *E.T.*, with Elliott riding a flying bicycle across the pale full moon.

"What's the latest?" he asked, flipping the salmon.

I glanced down at my phone to send a text message.

"Sorry, what?"

"It's okay," he said. "You're a busy man."

"No, it was just that one thing. Sorry, I'm here now.

"I hung out with Toby last night," I said, stuffing my phone into my back pocket. "He gave you a nice compliment, said you're better around young people than just about any dad he knows."

"Ha! The younger they are, the less fucked up they are." We sat at his table, a rectangular glass slab that looked like a real bitch to lug home from the Flea. He plunged his fork into the salmon and gobbled a bite.

On an adjacent wall, ET had recently hung a framed poster of *Steel Heel*, the movie he made when I was young. When I commented on the new art, he said he put it up to remind himself that he had made a feature film. "Success isn't measured in currency," he said. "It's measured in completion."

After a few minutes of catching up, I reminded ET about the time I cheated on my math test and my switch to homeschool.

"Did you feel railroaded by that move?" I asked.

"Homeschool taught you fortitude," he said, brushing it off. "Taught you time management skills. You're a self-starter, and your mom put in the work. You know what your mother used to do? She would flip a penny and, depending on whether it was heads or tails, take you on a walk in a different direction around the neighborhood. That's a pretty cool thing to do."

I wondered if ET really felt that way.

His point was valid. Through the homeschool years, my mom put in thousands of hours to work with me on a range of real-life projects, many of which focused on environmental activism. I learned to research, set my own deadlines, and pick up the phone to call experts—a skill that comes in handy when attempting a podcast or book. But my homeschooling also came with a slew of conspiracies that took years for me to untangle. Everything has trade-offs.

"Well, I feel like I was kinda fucked up to you through those years," I fumbled, stabbing at the pink fish. I looked down the hall to my old room. The place where I slammed a door in his face and coolly said that I respected my stepdad more than him. I set down my fork and scratched the back of my neck. "I'm really sorry."

"Nothing to be sorry about." He coughed, and his rusty eyes found a pine tree outside the window. I followed his gaze to the swaying conifer, and we both looked to the tree. After a long moment, my focus shifted back inside the house to a popcorn kernel at the base of a lamp at the end of the table. I squinted at the yellow kernel.

"Um, Dad, is that a tooth?"

"Sure is. Maybe I'll drill a hole through the center and turn it into a necklace." The tooth was the color of spoiled milk, yanked from the root.

"Is that *your* tooth?"

"Dentist finally pulled my wisdom tooth," he said, still bemused by the tree. "Because I'm such a wise guy."

I wasn't sure if he heard my apology, but it was the best I could do. Storybook endings only happen in rom-coms. In real life, apologies are often clumsy, unreceived, and end with the sight of a decaying tooth.

CHAPTER 18

What's a hobby of yours? (past or present)

AFTER LUNCH, WE WALKED TO HIS BACKYARD, HIS KINGDOM, a gazebo draped in vines, overlooking a small pond with lily pads and squat palm trees. We sat in two lattice chairs inside the gazebo, I uncoiled the microphone cords, and we started our interview. Humans are full of peculiar hobbies, and as interviewers, it's our job to draw them out. Parents can be bashful about these eccentricities, but *these* are the very qualities we celebrate at their funerals. During my interview with ET, when he told me the story of Muhammad Ali and the laughing mirror, we focused the conversation on his career as a filmmaker. For our second, I wanted to cover one of his great personal passions. He had emailed the photos from his life, I had written pages of questions, but ultimately the theme of the interview came down to a single word that I had circled: magic.

"Let's talk about magic," I said. "How did you get into it?"

ET scratched his chin. "Let's see, when I was eleven, my

mother came home with a chest of magic tricks from the 1930s. Beautiful, wooden, handcrafted magic tricks. Not like the plastic shit now. The box didn't come with instructions, so I just tinkered with it until I figured out each trick."

ET grew up in LA not far from where I live now, and spent a lot of time at Joe Berg's Magic Shop on Hollywood Boulevard.

"The moment you stepped through those doors, you were in a magic show. Floating balls, magic linking rings, and fire sticks I learned to swallow."

Soon he started performing at kids' birthday parties, and with the cash, his box of tricks grew. He threw animals into his act: rabbits, doves, ducks, and a guinea pig, which he would produce from thin air. *Five Dollars to See the Amazing Eric Thiermann!* The shy boy revealed his personality to the world in a tuxedo, top hat, and magic wand.

"Back then, you could get baby chicks for ten cents. I once did a birthday party and gave each kid a baby chick to take home. Their parents weren't too happy with me," he chuckled.

"Do any shows stand out for you?" I asked, nudging him to tell a story.

"I once performed for this tight-knit Hispanic family in Venice Beach. I did the show in a dimly lit living room, which makes everything more magical, and weaved together a one-hour show. The father walked up to me afterward, mesmerized, and slipped me an extra ten bucks."

"What made that show special?" I asked.

"The look of revelation on this guy's face," he said. "The key to life is finding moments of revelation. It keeps me going. To me, that's magic."

ET performed hundreds of events all the way through high school. When he was a sophomore, he ran for student body vice president at Santa Monica High School on a dare. In a packed auditorium of fifteen hundred students, he threw his speech on the ground and shouted, "I don't need this speech!"

The speech levitated back into his hand. The audience roared.

"My opponent started his speech by leading the school through a silent meditation...talk about a snooze fest."

In the campaign leading up to ET's landslide victory, his challenger ran on the slogan *You Can't Pull a President Out of a Top Hat.*

"Free publicity." ET gave a toothy grin.

During his reelection speech the next year, ET faced his entire school, stood to the side of the embossed wooden podium, pulled a handkerchief from his pocket, and wiped his forehead.

"I hope to turn the sweat and hard work that goes into creating a productive student government into something beautiful."

He threw the white handkerchief toward the audience, and it turned into a dove. The panicked bird flapped its wings around the perimeter of the auditorium, then landed obediently at his feet.

"Holy shit, I thought. I can't believe that worked!"

When ET graduated high school in 1964, he had his sights set on a radical new college nestled in a redwood grove. It was the first year UC Santa Cruz opened, and when he submitted his application, he led with the story of the election speech and the magic dove. Despite his B-minus GPA, the admissions board admired his chutzpah and let him in. In his first year of college, he bought a Mamiya Sekor single-lens reflex camera and ambled around the light-speckled forest, stepping over banana slugs, snapping shots and developing his own film. A girl from the yearbook committee solicited ET for his photography services. He agreed, and she gave him a list of scenes to shoot. It was his first media gig. When the yearbook came out a year later, 90 percent of the images were his.

"It was a total rush. A total rush."

The assignment was mostly portrait photography, so ET enticed the students to hang from rafters, stand on their heads, and climb out windows.

"In one shot, I captured three rows of guys wearing formal attire, and in the middle of the last row was a stark naked woman. I thought it was a classic shot, but I took it to the editor, and she said, 'I don't know if this is gonna fly,' so the editor took it to the faculty advisor, who took it to the provost, who took it to the chancellor, who made us tape a photo of a cow over the naked woman!"

When the fiftieth anniversary of UC Santa Cruz finally rolled around, ET reprinted the original image and cut a hinge on the picture so the alumni could toggle between the cow and the naked woman.

The summer after the yearbook came out in 1965, ET picked up a film camera and took it to Europe. He landed in Belgium, bought a motorcycle, and rode through France, Holland, Switzerland, Germany, Austria, Yugoslavia, Italy, Spain, and Morocco. One day, he was walking down a cobblestone street in France and dreamt up a movie about a group of strange characters who were invited to a picnic in an open field but didn't know who had invited them.

"It was a stupid little story. But suddenly, I stopped because I realized I had been daydreaming for hours, and I couldn't remember where the hell I was. Nothing else has ever had that kind of power over me. I lost my sense of self and was just in the flow. That's when I decided to become a filmmaker."

"Anything else?"

He zipped up his jacket as droplets of mist started to cling to it. "It's just interesting how a random choice like running for student body president on a dare can take your life in exceptional directions. You know, I met Harry Houdini once."

"You met Harry Houdini!?" I looked at the recorder to make sure we were still going.

"Yeah, he came by the magic store and performed. Just incredible. He took a buzz saw and cut a woman's body in half."

"How old was Houdini?"

"At least eighty-five, but man, he was as sharp as a knife." I conjured an image of my dad as a boy witnessing the most famous magician of all time in his final act of life.

"Wait, didn't Houdini die from a ruptured appendix when he was like fifty?"

ET paused, and the lines between his bushy eyebrows wrinkled a touch.

"Right. I meant Harry Blackstone."

CHAPTER 19

What's one lesson your parents taught you that you passed down to me?

I RECEIVED A TEXT FROM MY MOM: "FOSTER GOT SHINGLES in his cornea. We're going to the doctor now." Next, an image of someone mildly resembling my stepdad came through. The man had a sunken face and sclera the color of dragon fruit. The shingles escalated to a detached retina, and Foster underwent emergency surgery. In order for the retina to reattach during recovery, he needed to lie face down on a massage table, unmoving, for two weeks straight.

I drove to the house on the hill to check in on him.

"My iPhone finally recognized my face!" he bragged as he lay face down on a massage table, watching a tennis match on his tablet.

"That's funny," I said. It really was.

I watched the two of them that day, my mom shuffling around favoring her right hip, Foster mostly still, mortality in the air. At lunch before our interview, my mom and I sat on her patio, purple pillow under her butt, wind chimes the only sound to break the stillness of the day. She told me how helpful it was to have a partner in the last quarter of life, how sweet Foster had been to her during her recovery, and what an honor it was to take care of him now.

"He has a great attitude," she said, "and that's everything."

Since my last visit, she had officially stepped away from Thrive. My siblings' kids were growing fast, and she wanted to spend more time being a grandmother and less time orchestrating the revolution. While on a Reddit forum, I saw an IT guy write that he successfully yanked his own mother out of the rabbit hole by blocking propaganda websites on her router. By making it inconvenient to find those websites, she simply found new interests. I never went that far, but I did notice that my mom's new fascination with death had diverted her attention away from a quest to find free energy. To encourage this interest, I bought her a simple black-and-white calendar with four thousand small circles. Each circle represents one week of her life, and every Friday, she colors one in.

"After Richard died of cancer," she continued as we sat on her patio overlooking the scalloped coast of Monterey Bay, "we spread his ashes out to sea. In retrospect, I wish we hadn't done that because the ocean is so vast and unreachable; it's been difficult to locate a place where I can feel his spirit."

Richard was my grandfather. He died long before I was born, but I keep a photograph of him on a corkboard in my room, a handsome man in his forties, shirtless, with wavy brown hair, taking a drag off a cigarette. I had decided to focus our second interview on my mom's relationship with her parents. I wanted to know how her upbringing shaped her worldview.

***

"When did you spend the most time with your dad?" I asked as we started recording. I wanted her to locate a time and place mentally. Kids often have one or two activities they vividly remember doing with their parents, and encouraging them to expand on those activities can lead to colorful stories—not generalized platitudes.

"He would drive me an hour to school every morning. That's when we connected most. He had a red Thunderbird convertible, and we'd blow through the winding canyon road. On those drives, he would say, 'Don't believe everything you read.' He'd thump me on the head with two fingers and tell me to think critically."

I thought about butting in with another question, but I let her pause, take a sip of water, and continue. The Werner Herzog technique.

"I had a real spiritual yearning from a young age," my mom went on, "and my dad was the only one I could talk to about it. In those car rides, he would recite Thoreau to me, and make me memorize passages." Her eyes reached for the quote:

"I did not wish to live what was not life, living is so dear; nor did I wish to practice resignation, unless it was quite necessary. I wanted to live deep and suck out all the marrow of life."

She smiled, proud of her recall. "I've always liked the image of sucking the marrow out of life." Her family owned a three-bedroom house on the coast of Malibu. Back then, empty lots, open fields, and old beachfront homes defined the community of Northern Los Angeles. Not like the sterile McMansions of today. The house had portholes as windows. At high tide, waves lurched under the pilings, and the sound "wooshed" through the floorboards. Richard worked in PR and represented actors like Jack Lemmon (the Michael Cera of his generation), so my mom grew up through a fog of celebrity appearances at the cocktail parties her parents threw. Flowers, decadent appetizers, even Marilyn Monroe and John Kennedy showed up at a neighbor's party once.

"That," my mom said, "is how I know they were having an affair."

She brushed her hand through the side of her hair.

"Anyway, growing up was confusing," she said. "I saw a lot of screwed-up people become major Hollywood icons. It was hard to know what was real."

When my mom was twenty-six, Richard became ill with non-Hodgkin's lymphoma. The disease metastasized rapidly, and when the doctors told him there was nothing more they could do, they sent him home to die. As my mom sat beside Richard in his final days, she told him about her nagging cravings for hamburgers. "I was a vegetarian at the time. It was so strange."

"Maybe you're pregnant." Richard smiled. My grandfather never met my eldest brother, but while in hospice, he learned that his daughter would be a mother.

As Richard lay in bed, surrounded by his wife and children, a storm slammed into the coast. Waves surged through the home, and they were forced to evacuate. They put everything Richard owned into a moving truck and took it to another area for storage. The storm engulfed their childhood home, and my mom watched it rip from the pilings and float into the sea. Richard died shortly after. Then someone robbed the storage container, along with all of his possessions, erasing nearly every physical memory of my grandfather, all in one week.

"He visited me in a dream," my mom said. "It only happened once. It was years later. He was floating to heaven, and I shouted, 'Wait, Dad, I didn't get to ask you what I need to know in life.'

"He shouted back, 'Perseverance!'"

I thought about how memories can serve as reminders for how we should act in the future. Dreams are fleeting, but one that gives you identity can last forever.

"Can you describe your relationship with your mom?" I asked.

She scrunched her face. "We had a hard time."

CHAPTER 20

What's one thing you wanted to do differently from your parents when you raised me?

"SHE WAS A HIGH-FUNCTIONING ALCOHOLIC, AND I WAS A bit of a rebel. When I was young, I was a fast runner, and I could beat all the boys in sprints. My mom scolded me because girls weren't allowed to beat boys."

She paused with a look of regret, like she had been too harsh. "My brother just loved her. It's amazing how two children can interpret the same parent in totally different ways."

My grandmother lives in an assisted-living facility in Thousand Oaks, and not long ago, we visited for her ninety-ninth birthday. The facility was beige, with a terra-cotta exterior and ambient elevator music that leaked into every room. We walked down a hall into the memory care unit for patients with advanced Alzheimer's. In the common room, an employee stood in front of a whiteboard with an illustration of a bird. An old man yelled out, "Peacock!" The other players murmured their approval.

We met my grandmother in her room, where she sat in her wheelchair, wearing a white cotton long-sleeve shirt, eyes closed, a bobby pin in her hair.

"Hi," my mom said, rousing her slowly from a nap.

"Hi!" my grandmother's face lit up like a toothless jack-o'-lantern. "So good to see you."

"Hi, Grandma," I said, leaning down to eye level with her. "It's Kyle. Your grandson."

She studied my face for a long moment, leaned in, and responded, "What's up?"

I took a seat next to a long credenza with a vase of fake flowers and a photo collage of extended family members. In the corner of the room was a mechanical bed, set low to the ground, with a cream-colored comforter and waterproof sheets.

"Watch this," my mom whispered to me before greeting my grandmother a second time.

"Hi!"

Once again, my grandmother's face lit up. "Hi! So good to see you."

My mom gave her a head massage, and my grandmother dozed off again, thin white hair frizzy with bliss. Over the course of our visit, we introduced ourselves another half dozen times, each greeting as novel as the last.

"You get a lot of visits out of one visit," my mom said.

"Knock knock." The voice came from a nurse with an abundant smile. "Are we ready for lunch? We know how she loves her ice cream." My grandmother grinned mischievously, and we wheeled her into the cafeteria. Above the cafeteria kitchen was a sign that read *Meals and memories are made here.*

A bit of a stretch if you ask me.

"WHAT KIND OF ICE CREAM DO YOU LIKE?" I shouted into her ear.

"I like 'em all," she whispered back. When the ice cream arrived, she scooped the cup with vim, then her blue eyes flashed to a big-boned nurse standing in the corner, and back to me. "Look at the size of that woman's ass," she said benignly, then licked her spoon.

When my grandmother first showed signs of Alzheimer's, my mom asked what it felt like. She said, "I try to reach for words, but they're just too high." These days, she's done reaching and does best when conversations stay in the present—look at the blue jay, here's a head scratch, time for ice cream. A perk of Alzheimer's was that she simply forgot about brandy, switching instead to the sugar rushes of ice cream. After lunch, it was nap time. My mom and I hoisted her into bed. She rolled my grandmother's pant leg up to the knee, softly squeezing her calf the way she might a toddler.

"Mmm, feels good," my grandmother muttered before nodding off.

* * *

Back in the interview, the sun was going down. As our second of three interviews came to a close, I looked out the window and watched the sun crown the bay before disappearing behind the horizon.

"You know," said my mom, "I spent way too long wishing she was the mother I wanted rather than being grateful for the mother she was."

"What led to that insight?"

She laughed. "Psychedelics."

CHAPTER 21

What's one thing we have in common?

EVER SINCE MY MOM STEPPED AWAY FROM THRIVE, FOSTER downsized the operation. He now writes from a personal blog a few days a week. The last time I went to the blog, the top post had a pithy meme of a 1950s woman with a coffee cup and the line: "Not That We're Keeping Track or Anything...But Conspiracy Theories Are Up Thirty-Seven to Zero."

There's a scene in the movie *Walk the Line* where the music producer tells a young and aspiring Johnny Cash that if he was hit by a truck, splayed out in the gutter dying, and only had time to sing one last song—one song—to let God know how he felt about his time here on earth, one song to sum him up, he wanted to hear *that* song. Like most decent ideas, it smacked me on the forehead with its simplicity. It was a question, one I should have asked at the beginning of this project: What is the one piece of audio I will want after Foster is gone?

The framing of the question released the pressure valve on the whole project. It lightened things up. I didn't need to capture his *whole* life story, just one thing I could listen back to fifty years from now. What's your version of this? A lullaby your mom sang to you? A poem or baking recipe?

Our thread has always been athletics.

Before Thrive, Foster was a Division I athlete in both hockey and tennis. He later worked as a sports psychology coach, hired by NFL players, synchronized swimmers, and tennis pros. He trained in energy control and mindset. I was an early teen when he shared these powerful concepts with me, and when the time is right, I want to teach these concepts to my future kids, likely after he's gone. So I crafted a new interview, one that focused exclusively on our shared love of athletics. For some, sports is a hobby, but for Foster they cut much deeper. When he was a boy, his own father told him, "People are going to ask you for things for the rest of your life." No one pities a child with a trust fund, but there is a burden to being born on third base. Like having famous parents, or staring at your reflection through a funhouse mirror, Foster has navigated this warped existence from birth. But athletics are the ultimate meritocracy. The scoreboard is always honest, and Foster pursued sports with ferocity.

Once Foster's eye healed, I invited him on a hike not far from his house. The soil was rich, the color of charcoal, and as our shoes sank into the earth, moss clawed toward us from exposed overhangs. Petrichor still hung in the air from a rain shower the day before, and spiderwebs stretched across redwood branches in the flickering light. Foster wore blue jeans, a plain T-shirt, and a cowboy hat. He took slow, controlled steps on account of his eye. We were careful with our conversation, testing each topic like a foothold. He asked about my writing process. I asked about his.

We returned to his house after the hike. I made ginger tea, set up the audio gear, and pressed record.

* * *

"Let's start with athletic anxiety," I said. "How do you deal with it?"

Foster cleared his throat and scooted his chair close to the microphone. He slumped his shoulders, which still held power despite his age, resting his forearms on the table. He cleared his throat again and looked at me. His right eyelid was still droopy from the infection.

"Would you like my answers short, medium, or long?" After two documentaries and hundreds of hours on camera, Foster was a media veteran.

"Medium," I said.

"Great.

"I used to have an aikido teacher who told me, 'It's okay to have butterflies. Just make sure they fly in formation.' Anxiety is eagerness without breath. It's nothing more than extra energy to harness."

"Do you have any techniques to harness anxiety?"

"I once worked with a young woman who was a synchronized swimmer," said Foster. "The sport is incredibly demanding. You need to hold your breath upside down for long periods of time without breaking formation. The girl had already passed out twice and was terrified she might drown. I taught her this warm-up technique, and she went on to win the national championship the following year."

He righted his posture.

"The technique involves three basic levels: center, weight underside, and extended qi. First, imagine all the light of the universe plunging into your stomach, two inches below your navel. This helps you take those anxious thoughts and actively call in energy from the universe."

I imagined warm light filling into the vertical scar down my belly.

"Next, weight underside. This grounds your antenna." He told me to start at the top of my head and relax my jaw, shoulders, belly, and groin all the way down my legs until I noticed my feet. As he spoke, I felt my feet root into the carpet.

"Third, extend qi," He moved his hands slowly through the air like he was wielding a staff. He instructed me to extend my arms forward and imagine laser beams shooting out of the tips of my fingers, penetrating the walls and over the horizon.

"How should an athlete go about tackling bad habits?"

"Powerful question. Do you have any examples?"

"When I surf, I have a bad habit of standing up too tall and losing balance. When I see myself on camera, I sort of still feel like I suck after all these years."

I forced a chuckle, but he gave me a serious look.

"The most critical habit to break is language. You said, 'I still suck.' That's literally how you sustain a bad habit. Now, it may be true that in the past you've had this tendency to stand up too tall on your surfboard, but that's only true about your last session. It's not true right now. The key is to talk about your bad habits in the past tense, then create a game plan for how to tackle them in the next session. And when you do break the habit, even once, acknowledge yourself. This starts to build a positive new narrative."

Foster told me about a tennis coach named Tim Gallwey, who wrote a book called *The Inner Game of Tennis*. He met Gallwey at a couple of conferences, and when they talked, Gallway explained that every athlete plays from either Self One or Self Two. When it's game point and your opponent is serving, Self One hopes he'll double fault. Self Two says, "Give me your best shot."

We talked about sports a while longer, and then finished.

"Thanks for the wisdom," I said earnestly.

He gave a boyish smile. "Thanks for your curiosity."

"How about a game of Ping-Pong?"

"Love to."

The air was cool in his garage, and more than fifty excess binders framed the walls, as well as a few old surf trophies from my teens. In the center of the garage was a Ketler Ping-Pong table, a sleek green surface with white lines marking the perimeter.

Foster took the side against the garage door, and light spilled through the plexiglass window, silhouetting his frame. After a few net balls, we got into rhythm, my lefty forehand against his righty backhand. "This is great rehab for my eye," Foster exclaimed.

As we rallied, I took a risk and asked what he had been up to recently. He said he had been researching vaccines. Apparently, new vaccines contained microchipped antennas and could be controlled with joysticks.

"Interesting," I said. "Crosscourt now. Let's see how long we can keep this rally going."

CHAPTER 22

Have you ever had a near-death experience? What's the story?

EVER SINCE I HAD STARTED THIS PROJECT, DEATH HAD BEEN on my mind. The whole thing had turned into a strange exercise in memento mori, the ancient stoic practice of reflecting on mortality as a way to live with more purpose. I had made a habit of journaling a few pages after each interview. If the shingles had spread to Foster's brain, I would have regretted not sitting down with him, not taking the time to find our common denominator. Death is the ultimate perspective shift, and as the pages filled, one word appeared, and along with it, a memory that would help me as I prepared for the final interview with my mom. The word was Mexico.

Death came as a pang in my side. The sort you get from running on a full stomach. I was fourteen in a thatched hut in Mexico when I felt the alien bulge an inch above my pubic bone. It was night, still a sticky eighty-five degrees, and a single fan swung lazily between my friend Nick and me, who lay in his own puddle of sweat on the other side of the room. Beyond the hut, I heard the electric hum of the jungle. An endless expanse of muddy rivers and dank fecundity, punctuated every minute or so with the clap of waves against sand.

By morning, I was in the fetal position, writhing.

The door opened, light spilled onto the cement floor, and my dad walked in. "Montezuma's revenge," he consoled. "No fun at all."

ET sat on the edge of my bed, felt my forehead, and told me to sleep it off. Food poisoning blows through like a tropical storm. I'd be on the other side of it soon.

Toby was on the surf trip too. He gave me a fist bump and told me not to shit myself. The swell was building, so they equipped me with a bag of crackers and a jug of water, and set off for the day. When they returned later that afternoon, ET asked if I had shit. No. Puked? Also no. That night, a hand gripped my intestines like a gardener pulling weeds. I whimpered and moaned, clutched my pillow, and quietly cried.

"I think something's wrong with Kyle," Nick told my dad on the second morning. "Like, it could be bad."

The nearest clinic was two hours away. I lay down in the back seat of the rental car. Upside down, palm trees blurred at a slow shutter speed. Burn piles flashed. Shapes formed in the smoky sky, and every speed bump felt like a full-body concussion. We pulled into the dirt lot outside the clinic, and I held my dad's arm as I stepped out of the car. The clinic was hot, crowded, and smelled like antiseptic. The man in the seat next to me had blood-soaked bandages wrapped across his head. Mexican families fanned themselves with pop culture magazines.

"Toby!" ET ran back to the car. "Toby, get the fuck in here!"

My condition had worsened as I doubled over in the waiting

room chair. Toby spoke better Spanish than ET, and we needed a translator. A nurse put me on a gurney and rolled me into the back room; a long, fluorescent hallway illuminated a uniform row of patients in critical condition. The nurse pricked me with an IV, put a needle in the injection port, and started to push down. Another nurse walked up behind her and casually said, "No, no, not him. Over there."

"Ah," said the first nurse. She removed the needle and plunged it into the man next to me.

My dad went white.

After another hour, the doctor arrived, a stethoscope wrapped around his neck. When he pressed on my stomach with two fingers, I nearly passed out. He told Toby, who translated to ET, that I had ruptured my appendix and needed emergency surgery "ahora."

An appendectomy is a common surgery. The doctor cuts a small, vertical incision in the belly and removes the swollen appendix. But in my quixotic endeavor to tough it out, I had let the small sack rupture. Bacteria now spilled into my abdominal cavity. Soon, I would go into septic shock and meet a rather unpleasant death. Worse still, my surf trip would be over.

At age fourteen, I still failed to grasp the severity of the situation, even as the doctor drew invisible lines across my stomach with his finger.

"So I'll be out of the water for one week?" I attempted in broken Spanish. "Maybe two?"

The doctor told my dad that in my critical condition, he would need to open me up, remove my intestines, wash my stomach cavity with saline solution, reinsert my guts, and sew me back together again.

"We can do surgery here," the doctor said. "But the room es, como se dice...no finish."

* * *

A country away, my mom jogged on a dirt trail in Santa Cruz, drinking in cool California air. Wilder Ranch is a state park of sinuous trails that guide runners up hills laced with delphinium and clover into canopied forests of Douglas fir, oak, and redwood, spitting them out at a bluff that overlooks the Pacific. She ran by an embossed wooden bench dedicated to someone who had died, and like a blast of warm air, was overcome by a sudden thought: *Something happened to Kyle.*

Maybe it was a coincidence. I can't prove anything. But I'm open to the idea that humans have the ability to perceive one another beyond our five senses. On the bench, she cried, heaving and guttural. When she got home, she told Foster about it.

* * *

Meanwhile, I was in an ambulance, zigzagging through traffic. ET sat in the back with me while Nick and Toby trailed us in the rental car. We were en route to Colima, three hours away, where I would go under the knife. My mom's phone rang. Toby was on the other line.

"Hi, can you hear me? Kyle's in an ambulance. We're going into surger—." The phone died.

It was hours before he could make the next call. During this time, my mom assembled a war room of American doctors. I'm surprised she didn't get the president on the line.

When Toby called a second time, we were in Colima Hospital. I was on another gurney, in another fluorescent room, in and out of consciousness. ET and my mom considered putting me on a plane to do the surgery closer to home, but as every hour inched by, poison leached through my bloodstream. I needed surgery yesterday.

A nurse finally rolled me into surgery, and masked men and women stood over me. Next to my head, silverware gleamed in the light. As I lay on the cold operating table in a white, backless gown, I gritted my teeth and focused my attention far away to the Mentawais in Indonesia, the tropical island chain I planned to visit as soon as I turned eighteen.

The anesthesiologist injected something into my IV, and I saw the liquid snake down the needle into my vein. My vision blurred, and when I opened my eyes, I ran my tongue across the inside of my cheek and felt cotton. I lifted my head off the pillow to get a look at my stomach, but my gown kept my incisions hidden.

For the next week, I wasn't in a condition to travel, and ET read me *Harry Potter and the Goblet of Fire*. The hospital was muggy without air-conditioning, so a grandmother taking care of a family member in the bed next to me dabbed my body with rubbing alcohol to cool me down. The doctor released me on the seventh day. The bill for my entire visit was ninety dollars US. ET slid a hundred-dollar bill across the counter and used the change to pay for the cab to the airport.

ET dropped me off at my mom's house that night. I hadn't taken a real shower in days, so I washed off before bed. When I stepped out of the shower, dripping and naked, I wiped off the steaming mirror and saw the full view of my reflection. Slowly, I peeled off the bandages, unveiling a foot of vertical stitches, belly button to pubic bone, and two stinted tubes out my abdomen to release pus.

I heard a knock on the door, wrapped a towel around my waist, and opened it. My mom stood in the doorway in her pajamas. At fourteen, I was already taller than her. Her eyes stopped at my stitches. She flashed my incision a tight smile, hugged me, and, with her head resting on my shoulder, whispered, "You smell so infected."

CHAPTER 23

What's a hard truth you've had to accept?

"HAVE YOU HELPED ANYONE DIE LATELY?" I ASKED OVER THE phone.

"Ha ha ha! You know I don't help people die," the voice clarified. "I'm just *with* people when they die."

"Right," I said. "That's what I meant."

I was in LA at the time of the call. Between quick jaunts north to push the interview project along, I had been swept up in my own career, crafting ad campaigns for companies that wanted to live forever. Rachel, on the other hand, had made the move from regular old hospice to pediatric hospice. She worked with terminal patients ages zero to twenty-four. Apparently, they were short on staff. (Can't fathom why.)

"What's it like being with dying kids?" I asked, slipping in my AirPods to take a walk around the block.

"Kids tend to be better at dying than adults. They've been less indoctrinated into the idea that death is wrong. Their attitudes are more like, 'Alright, this is what we're gonna do.'" I was struck by how she used the word "better." Like cooking a soufflé or working on your golf swing, Rachel saw dying as just another skill, an ability to improve with practice.

"Did you interview your mom?" she asked.

"I did two, but I'm planning to go back one more time."

"How did the first ones go?"

"Good, I think. I don't know. It's just the conspiracy theory shit. It pisses me off that she's wasting her life on this stuff. And it's insane how big it's gotten. It makes me feel like..." I paused, standing on the corner of my street as a driver in a matte-black Tesla sped through the stop sign. "Like we're not gonna make it as a species."

Before COVID, conspiracy theories were still on the fringe of culture. It was minor-league baseball. Only a few people knew the teams. But when COVID hit, conspiracy theories exploded across the internet—and into surf culture. On a recent swell at the San Lorenzo Rivermouth, a wave at the center of Santa Cruz that attracts all the best surfers from both the Eastside and Westside, a shouting match had erupted in the water. The subject: chemtrails.

"Hmm," Rachel said knowingly. "It's good you're aware of your anger. It means you still care about the world, and your mom.

"Can I ask you a question?" she continued.

"Go for it." I crossed the street and kept walking.

"How does your mom view the way she lives?"

"Oh, she's living in her truth." The answer came quickly, and I chuckled when I said it aloud. The ethic she imbued most in me as a child—to be your own person no matter the pressures of culture—was the same quality that magnetized her to conspiracy theories.

"So, from her perspective, she's doing the best she can?"

"For sure."

"And interviewing her is helping you understand some of the reasons why she lives the way she does?"

"I think so."

"Kyle, have you heard of a woman named Tara Brach?"

I had. Her book *Radical Acceptance* had been collecting dust on my shelf for the past year, but I hadn't so much as cracked it open.

"Acceptance," Rachel said. "That's the magic word."

I feared where she was going next. *Buddhist assignments*.

"I've seen a lot of kids who haven't dealt with the issues they have with their parents, and it can seep out as anger during hospice. I recommend the book to anyone who feels unresolved.

"It has a self-compassion exercise called RAIN. When you feel yourself becoming loathsome and need to find compassion, follow these steps: Recognize what is happening. Allow the experience to be there, just as it is. Investigate with interest and care. Nurture with self-compassion.

"Practice accepting small things," she finished. "It will prepare you to accept big things—and ultimately the biggest thing."

CHAPTER 24

What scares you but is good for you?

THE FIRST TIME I EVER SURFED MAVERICKS, THE WELL-known big wave an hour north of Santa Cruz, it was a gusty fall afternoon, and the waves were about thirty feet. The reef at Mavericks is shaped like a finger. Between October and April, swells fan across the ocean—spinning off the coast of Japan, the Aleutian Islands, or the Kamchatka Peninsula. Buoys rise and fall, measuring the swell's height, angle, and velocity like a stethoscope, taking the pulse of the Pacific Ocean. When the raw wave energy finally makes contact with the reef at Mavericks, half a mile offshore, the ocean folds in on itself, detonating an explosion that can spit white water nearly a hundred feet in the air. The power is akin to watching a volcano erupt or a glacier calve. When paddling up the face of a wave this size, all you can do is take slow, steady breaths and control what you can, which is very little.

"If you get caught in the rocks," my friend Tyler told me as we walked out to the beach in wetsuits, our feet crunching against the dirt path, "take your leash off and hold it in your hand so you don't get wrapped around the rocks and die." Noted. Don't get wrapped around the rocks and die.

As we walked, seagulls and pelicans circled overhead, and sailboats bobbed safely in the Pillar Point harbor to our left. I didn't own a big wave board at the time, so Tyler let me borrow his. It was a specialty blade, nine feet long, heavy, designed to cut through water at top speeds. These boards are referred to as "guns." An early big wave pioneer named Pat Curren said, "If you want to hunt elephants, you need an elephant gun," and the name stuck. The paddle out took us over half an hour as we punched through successively rougher white water, sweating through thick wetsuits, on the way to the peak.

I decided to catch a wave right away. *This is just another day of surfing. Don't overthink it.* After maybe a half hour of waiting, a set approached. I turned and paddled. It was absolutely the biggest wave I had ever attempted. But, as I stood up, I felt something brush my feet. The onshore wind had crumbled in the lip, white water caught my ankles, and suddenly, I was surfing down the wave. Without my surfboard.

I remember the violence, pressure, and a whining sound as my ears struggled to equalize on the way down.

Then silence.

It's called "tombstoning." A surfer gets sucked so deep underwater that their leash, which is attached to their ankle, stretches to maximal capacity, and only the tip of the surfboard nose remains visible, standing taught, unmoving, amid a graveyard of foam, like a tombstone.

It was, without a doubt, one of the best experiences of my life.

* * *

You see, I'm depressed.

Or rather, I have feelings of depression. I'm working on framing it this way. I have a friend who has lower back problems. He'll lift a box without bending his knees or sleep on his stomach, his back will spasm, and he'll spend the next few days laid up in bed, unable to work or tie his shoes. Depression is like that. A disk slips in my mind, and suddenly, I feel profoundly alone. I have no friends. No skills. No purpose. None of these thoughts are true, of course, and the best I can do is ride it out, hurl myself into cold water, and pray that tomorrow will be better. I've never been suicidal, just sad. Prone to vicious inner monologues and melancholy. My mom once described me as having "achievement bulimia." No matter the accolade, my self-esteem was starved.

But on the day I skipped down that wave at Mavericks and was sucked to the bottom of the Pacific, I was forced into a very personal conversation. *You got this, Kyle. You got this.* That was all I said. And when I came up for air, veins coursing with adrenaline, I felt a little more self-actualized. A little more durable.

Over the years, I've become friends with a lot of big wave surfers, and learned that the community is full of quiet depressants. Extreme-sports athletes often use adrenaline to treat their symptoms. Sometimes I look around the lineup at Mavericks and imagine that we're all in line at a drugstore, hands out at nature's Prozac dispenser.

It's not that Mavericks cured my depression. It didn't. But over the past decade of surfing waves that can top fifty feet and training for the falls, it's given me tools that can soften the blow. Big wave surfing is a focal point. Simple and physical. When I'm feeling slothful, it gives me a reason to swim, do breathwork, and meditate. After years of surfing Mavericks, and other big waves around the world, I was invited to compete in the prestigious Mavericks contest, a surreal honor.

* * *

For most of my life, my mom has been one of the only people I could talk to about my depression. Each time my name appeared on her phone, it was a game of Russian roulette.

"Hi, are you okay?" she would hastily answer. No idea if the voice on the other end of the line would be chipper, fresh back from the beach, calling to tell her I loved her. Or would I barely be able to speak? Would she need to cancel her meetings? Would she need to make me promise?

"I think you need intensity to find presence," she reflected after I told her I had surfed Mavericks. Rather than try to dissuade me from surfing dangerous waves, she got in my corner. We even made a list of things to do when I felt depressed: Go for a run. Take a cold shower. Journal one page. Go to a comedy show. Don't drink. That woman has grace like you wouldn't believe.

I say all this because interviewing your parents should come from a place of love, and if you can't make contact with that feeling, your interview will fail. I don't care how beautifully crafted your questions are. If you show up with retracted energy, your parents will mirror you.

When I interviewed my mom a third and final time, it was helpful to bifurcate her into two separate personalities. There's the conspiracy theorist, sure. The one on camera swimming in a thick custard of delusion. And there's my mom. The one who always met my depression with inquiry. The one who was an open channel through my darkest moments. That's the part I tried to speak to when sitting across from her during our last interview. Not just with my words, but my body language too. Only 7 percent of what we say is communicated through words. Tone, eye contact, posture, head nodding, keeping your hands visible on the table, and a genuine smile are how we really speak. Body language, like language, is a learned skill, and you can learn it too. Whatever part of your parents you can find love for, define it, even if it's small. Dad's cooking. Mom's knack for sewing Halloween costumes from scratch. Write it down, picture it, then think to yourself, "I love you." I know this sounds like some California hippie shit, which it totally is, but your tone, body language—and yes, energy—will all impact the result of your interview.

My mom has a green thumb, and when she was a little girl, a neighbor gave her radish seeds. Now, I don't know how much you know about radishes, but they are the cockroaches of plants, impossible to kill.

"You're such a talented gardener," the neighbor told my mom as she pulled the red bulbous roots from the soil.

After she and ET split, we moved to a small house where she transformed the yard from some forlorn dust bowl into a lush fantasia. Gophers avoid her garden, simply out of respect.

One day, a melittologist (bee researcher) was walking through the neighborhood. "What an impressive variety of species," he told my mom. When she moved in with Foster to the house on the hill, she made it her mission to turn the garden into a native bee utopia. In a citizen's effort to combat colony collapse disorder, she planted lavender, salvias, lemon trees, tangerine trees, and grevillea.

"The neighbors might hate me now," she'd say as clouds of manure trailed the dump trucks en route to her house, blanketing the road with a pungent aroma. "But they'll be grateful when these artichokes are ready to harvest."

These days, her garden doesn't buzz. It roars.

She stayed in touch with the melittologists, and some days, dozens of Berkeley students can be found in her garden, hunched over her roses with tweezers and microscopes, identifying her seventy-eight species of native bees pollinating her flowers. From tiny black bees easily mistaken for gnats to puffed-up bumblebees, legs heavy with pollen, her garden may single-handedly rebound the species.

My relationship with my mom is layered, and it's easy to let darkness eclipse the light. When I read the news and see legions of conspiratorial-minded people in America and think that my mom has been infected by this virus, it gets me down. But as interviewers, it's our job to find our parents' humanity. Conjure a moment that makes you smile and return to that place again and again. I picture my mom in her garden, boots in the soft earth, fresh kale overflowing from the wicker basket in her hand, a satisfied smile on her face. This is the mom I can talk to about my pain. This is the mom who is also my friend. And it makes me smile to know that the smells and sounds that will always remind me of her, are manure and a swarm of bees.

CHAPTER 25

What is your most painful memory?

TALKING ABOUT TRAUMA AND USING THIS PROJECT TO explore pain in your parents' lives is not requisite. There are no grades here. All you have are your questions, a recorder, and the subtle push and pull between how deep you want to dig and how much your parents are willing to share. But as Brené Brown said in her newsletter, "An experience of collective pain does not deliver us from grief or sadness; it is a ministry of presence. These moments remind us that we are not alone in our darkness and that our broken heart is connected to every heart that has known pain since the beginning of time." So if your parents are ready to talk, and you are ready to listen, you may gain a sense of compassion that can only arise from digging through the muck.

Before the last interview, I asked my mom if she was willing to talk about her childhood trauma, and finished the request by saying, "Totally no problem if you'd rather not." She agreed. My only job was to stay present, lean in with love, and gently guide the interview.

If your parents agree, you can say things like, "Keep going. What else do you remember? How does it feel to talk about this? Or tell me more about *blank* detail in the story." When they finish, thank them, and tell them it was a really brave thing to do.

Because it was.

While covering this terrain with my own mom, we dedicated an entire interview to it. You do not want to breeze through this stuff. If you only have the option to record one interview with your parent, I recommend taking a ten-minute break after you cover the difficult material. Stop recording, stand up, walk around the block, then sit back down to finish the interview, or save it for the end.

* * *

She had told me bits and pieces of the story years ago, but never in detail. It's not something she likes to talk about.

"Ready?"

"Ready."

"Okay, will you tell me the story of Juarez?" She nodded.

"Yeah, so that incident. It was July 12, 1965, and I was thirteen years old. Back then, we had Renaissance fairs on these big fields. I was on the outskirts of the field at these animal stalls. No one was around, and this guy came up. I remember thinking, huh, this doesn't feel good. But like most girls who are raped, I thought, well, I don't want to seem impolite, so I'll stay here and be uncomfortable. I remember I couldn't scream. I tried to scream, and no sound came out."

When it was over, she ran home, took a shower, and washed the blood off her back.

My grandfather, Richard, had non-Hodgkin's lymphoma at the time, the cancer that would return years later to take his life. When I asked why she didn't tell him what had happened, she said she was worried that the news would kill him.

Two months after the incident, her parents were throwing a neighborhood barbeque. An older friend of hers, who was seventeen at the time, asked if she was okay. She told him what had happened. The next day, he drove her to Planned Parenthood.

In the summer of 1965, abortion in California was illegal, so she invented a story that she and her friend were going on a trip to Tahoe. Instead, they found an abortion clinic in Juarez, Mexico, and booked her a plane ticket. When she landed in Juarez alone, she met a man at the airport who was part of an underground network of abortion clinics that American girls flew to in those days. My mom didn't speak Spanish, so the only way for the man to identify her was by her outfit.

She chose a favorite pink floral dress.

"I had never been out of the country," she said. "I had never seen chickens in the streets or kids dressed in rags. It was a completely different world."

When she arrived at the clinic, a man sat her down in line with the other women, some of whom were in their third trimester. The clinic had only a few rooms, and as she and the other girls waited, cockroaches crawled the white walls.

"He was the epitome of a hungry, creepy, fat guy who reminded me of the big bad wolf," she said. "He smirked and picked me to come in first. No weighing me. No checking to see if I had eaten before getting a complete dose of anesthesia."

When she awoke from surgery and was strong enough to stand, she put on her pink floral dress and, just as she had always been taught, folded the sheets and started to make her bed. Then, she stopped.

"I remember thinking, I'm not going to make this fucking bed."

* * *

As my mom sat across the table from me, headphones on, speaking into the microphone, I wanted to disassociate, change the subject, to her garden, to conspiracy, to anything but this. But I just listened, every so often asking if there was anything else she wanted to tell me.

"It was on that hospital bed in Juarez that I thought, *Fuck what I was taught about not rocking the boat*. I was in that situation because I didn't want to offend someone. I decided right then: I'm still alive, and I am never going to let this happen again. That belief was forged deep and strong."

When she finally arrived home from Juarez, she took off her floral dress and threw it in the trash.

In the years following the abortion, she had a great-aunt who died and left her some money. Before therapy was common, she used the cash to see a psychotherapist five days a week. She intuitively knew she had to deal with the trauma, so they talked, and talked, and talked. They relived the experience, but this time she screamed and got away.

"Through all the therapy, I found my voice," she said. "I realized that if only 51 percent of me felt strong, that was enough to act."

"How do you think that experience has shaped your life?" I asked.

"It's influenced everything, I'm sure," she said. "From protesting back in the Berkeley days to starting the homeless shelter. I will stand up to anyone trying to exert power over others."

I thought about *Thrive*. The woman on screen so willing to pick a fight against anyone she perceived as vying to exert control over others. I thought about how primal her reactions always were, how they seemed to come from her very center.

Eventually, she did tell her parents. An unexpected bill arrived from the hospital. Her mom brought it to her and said, "There's this hospital bill. I never knew you were in the hospital. Listen, I'm going to go take a nap, but when I get up, let's talk about it."

She called her therapist and asked what she should do. He told her to tell the truth.

"My dad cried," she said, wiping her eyes. "It was one of the only times I saw him cry."

As she finished the story, I didn't have any more questions, and a faint ambiance of the recorder padded the silence. Then, she finished our interview.

"I can honestly say that if I die today, I'm okay. I have lived my life and have never ventured so far that there are whole chunks I can't account for. If there's one thing I'm most proud of teaching my kids, it's to live your lives. Don't give in to the pressures to conform. It will rob you of your life."

"Is there anything you want me to remember after you're gone?" I asked.

She closed her eyes.

"I feel most sad when you waste your time in self-loathing,
and most grateful when you hold yourself in reverence,
to witness yourself as the hero of your story."

CHAPTER 26

What do you want more of from your kids?

THE NEXT DAY MY MOM CALLED. IT HAD BEEN MORE THAN fifteen years since she had seen me surf, and she wanted to come down to the beach and watch. I said of course, so we made a day of it. I loaded my car, and we drove up a stretch of coast between Santa Cruz and San Francisco, still mostly unmarked by development. To our right were strawberry fields, cattle grazing pastures, and redwood forests, and to our left was the Pacific Ocean, its surface shivering with bursts of wind.

"I was thinking about our last interview," my mom said.

"How do you feel about it?"

"I feel good. But Juarez was sixty years ago. That's not my whole story, you know."

I clicked my jaw reflexively. "Yeah, of course."

A few years back, a torrid lightning storm ignited the northern coast, and the mountains turned black with ash. We drove past a charred redwood tree standing tall on the side of the road. It looked like a wounded veteran back from war.

"What *is* your story?"

"For me"—she paused—"it's about coming home to myself."

"How do you mean?" I kept both hands on the wheel, and a gust of wind pushed against the car, causing us to drift before I righted us.

"I've been married five times," she said. "I became a mom straight out of college, and I spent a lot of time helping my husbands do *their* projects. I don't regret any of it. But for this last quarter of my life, I'm focused on myself. I'm finally getting to know *me* on another level."

The previous year, she traveled to Costa Rica for a series of ayahuasca ceremonies. She said drinking the psychedelic helped her slow down. I had noticed the energy shift in her. Less clenched. She might be the only person in the world for whom taking psychedelics resulted in fewer conspiracy theories.

She continued. "I know *Thrive* affected you. And I can see how some of our beliefs could come across as flagrant disregard for expertise." I clicked my jaw again, stayed quiet, and let her go on. It was the first time I had heard her say anything like this. "But I hope world affairs come second to our relationship."

I wanted to ask more but it didn't seem worth it to get into the weeds. It felt like trying to explain the Iraq war, a two-decades-long quagmire, one we were no longer fighting. I kept my hands on the wheel and said, "Makes sense." We had more important things to talk about.

We pulled off the highway and walked down a dirt path half a mile from the beach. Poison oak and tangled blackberry bushes rose up on either side of us. Worried she might get cold, my mom armed herself with a knitted beanie and navy-blue puffer jacket. I held a folded chair under one arm, my surfboard under the other, and a purple dry backpack slung around my shoulders. I wondered if the walk would be pushing it on account of her bionic hip and femur, but she bounded ahead, the dirt path crunching beneath her feet.

"You may be happy to know that I've been rucking," she boasted, showing me a photo of her with a weighted vest on. It looked like someone had superimposed a photo of a sweet old lady over a Navy SEAL.

We crossed a small creek that meandered in spaying fingers across the sand until it reached the sea. The air was a mix of briny mist, rotting kelp, and elephant seal shit. We found a spot in the corner of the beach and set up the chair for her. I put a towel around my waist and climbed into my wetsuit.

"Have fun," she said, binoculars holstered.

As I ran down the beach, raptors banked across the sky and nested along the pocked cliff. The water was in the low fifties, and each duck dive jolted me with an electric brain freeze. As I bobbed around in the lineup, I thought about the hours of interviews I had recorded with my mom. Three gigabytes of audio files, her voice encased in time like a fly in amber. Why had I spent so much time doing this? More than a year of my life, stuck in the past. I squinted into the harsh white light of the horizon for some saccharine answer, then laughed to myself at one possibility. "Because it's a good story." A set approached, and waves refracted off the cliff, joining together in A-frames, like two hands clasping in prayer. I chased one down and surfed it to shore, grunting with each top turn, surprised at how badly I wanted to impress my mom—despite the fact that she was blind to any difference between good and bad surfing. When the wave closed out, I looked to the beach. The giant blueberry waved back. As I paddled back out, my tone darkened. Was I exploiting her? My mom who had supported me through years of school and sports and depression. The guilt of splaying out my family for public consumption had finally hit. But there was another reason I had done this, and Derek Sivers wrote it best in *How to Live*: "You aren't supposed to be easy to explain. Putting a label on a person is like putting a label on the water in the river. It's ignoring the flow of time."

Yes, I had captured a few stories, but this was only part of her. Making a habit of asking my parents questions, with or without a recorder, felt like the real way to improve relationships. Questions are invitations to see our parents in the present tense. *Who are you today? I want to know.* They are a willingness to let ourselves be surprised, and a declaration that we care about the wisdom of elders in a culture obsessed with youth.

The sun fell behind the cliff, and my fingers were numb, so I rode one last wave to shore, scattering a fling of sandpipers as I jogged up the beach.

"Wow," said my mom as she stood up from her chair. "That looked like so much exercise."

I laughed, peeling off my wetsuit. I stuffed it into my backpack, water dripping from my nose. The sky had turned a brilliant bruised pink, fading behind a glassy curved sea.

"Where do these swells come from?" she asked. Her nose was rosy from the cold, and strands of gray hair spilled out of her beanie.

"Off the coast of Japan, likely."

"And you want the biggest waves because they let you go faster?"

"Yeah, that's generally true." I had never thought of it quite like that. "But you also want a wave with good shape so you can ride it longer."

"That's so interesting." She was directing the conversation to a subject I had a close relationship with and knew a great deal about.

"How did you feel out there?"

I told her I was nervous about making the interview project public. I patted sand off my feet and flipped my wet backpack around my shoulders. She held the foldable chair in her hand. I reached for the aluminum frame, and she offered it to me.

"Oh, I'm not worried." She gave a crooked grin. "Never hold back what you believe to be true."

CHAPTER 27

What are you most grateful for?

BEFORE DRIVING BACK TO LA, I MET ET AT TORTILLA FLATS, a cozy and colorful Mexican restaurant that serves lethal margaritas, throws Frida Kahlo look-alike contests, and seems to be in yearlong celebration of Día de los Muertos, the walls are covered with painted ceramic skulls and skeletons riding bicycles. The Reaper would feel right at home. I arrived a few minutes late, scanned the busy room, and spotted ET at a table in the corner. He waved to me.

"Hey, Mr. Dude," he said, then sniffled.

He looked older, the sunspots on his forehead had gained territory, and his widow's peak had thinned. He wore a faded green Patagonia jacket, the left arm covered with flecks of house paint.

"Did I get you that thing?" I asked, pointing to the jacket as I scooted into the booth.

"Oh, I always let my kids dress me. It's how I stay lookin' so stylish."

The waitress arrived and we ordered mole enchiladas.

"How's your book coming along?" he asked. "Is that the one about interviewing your parents?"

I told him it was nearly finished.

"That'll be a good one. You know, most kids think their parents are these oddball characters. We're just people. As soon as you can start treating them as people, you'll have such a better time."

We ate our mole enchiladas, and ET wiped his mouth with a napkin.

"Did I ever tell you the story of Joseph Heller, the guy who wrote *Catch-22*?"

"Remind me."

"So Heller wrote the wildly popular book *Catch-22*. He's at a billionaire's house on Shelter Island, and his pal, Kurt Vonnegut, informs Heller that their host, a hedge fund manager, makes more money in a day than Heller did on his entire novel. Heller responds, 'But I have something he will never have.' Do you know what that is?"

"Enough," we both mouthed.

"I got something for ya," ET said as we walked out of the restaurant. His Prius was parked on the street. Cold air cut the night, and a fingernail moon hung above. He opened the hatchback, patted around in the dark, and grabbed them.

"Size twelve, right?" In each hand, he held an iridescent camouflage running shoe. "Pretty cool, huh? Picked these babies up from the Flea for five bucks."

He handed me the hideously divine shoes. I admired them and carefully set them on the pavement. I stepped forward and wrapped my arms around his torso, bending my knees to make myself small, and placed my cheek on his collarbone. ET put his arms around my shoulders and rested his chin on the top of my head. He smelled like my dad. Cars drove past, and I heard muffled sounds of pedestrians walking by on the sidewalk. I felt his belly against mine, rising and falling.

"Man," he said after a final squeeze and scratch of the back. "That's one for the books."

Once you interview your parents, I would genuinely love to know how it goes. Email me one surprising, funny, or heartwarming thing you learned about them (and anything else you'd like to share). I'll read every one. You can email me at Thiermann@Substack.com.

My newsletter is also on Substack, and my podcast, *The Kyle Thiermann Show*, is in all the usual places.

Interview Checklist

PREINTERVIEW PREP

- **Contact your parents now:** Set the date. Figure out the rest later. Provide two or three time slots when you reach out.

- **Ask your parents to share photographs and other memorabilia, preferably in advance of the interview:** The items they choose to share will prompt questions and unlock memories.

- **Test your gear:** A low buzz in the microphone will bring shame to your ancestors.

- **Get the Audio-Technica ATR2500X-USB cardioid condenser USB microphone ($68):** This professional-grade microphone will do their stories justice. It plugs into your phone so you can record from the Voice Memos app, but the results will be noticeably crisper than just using your phone. I've personally tested a bunch of microphones, and this is the best one for the price.

- **Buy a foam screen ($4):** A foam screen fits over the microphone and will keep your parents from popping their Ps as they recount the story of when Peter Piper picked a peck of pickled peppers.

- **Check storage:** If you use the Voice Memos app on your iPhone, do you have enough memory? iPhones record voice memos using either lossless or compressed audio. If you use lossless, the audio file will take up two gigabytes per hour. If you use compressed, it will consume one hundred megabytes per hour. Lossless is for musicians. Compressed will be fine. Open settings, find Voice Memos, and make sure you're recording in compressed audio.

- **Recording remotely? Get Zoom Pro ($14):** You can cancel it the next day. Also, parents who use AirPods will sound better than they would speaking straight into the computer microphone.

- **Write at least ten shitty questions:** Set a twenty-minute timer on your phone and write as many questions as possible.

- **Go for bold questions:** If it's going to feel a little uncomfortable to ask, you're on the right track.

- **Are your questions too broad?:** Specificity, specificity, specificity! Break their lives into four chunks (childhood, young adult, adult with kids, empty nester) and write half a dozen questions for each stage.

- **Avoid questions that will get a yes or no response:** Rewrite these questions and insert words like story, moment, and why. What was the *moment* you decided to join the air force? Tell me the *story* of your first date with my mom. *Why* do you drink half a Sierra Nevada in the shower each morning?

- **Go for Deep Questions:** Move beyond the facts of their lives and into how they feel about their lives. "What did it feel like to...?" Thanks, Charles Duhigg.

- **Write questions that draw out stories from their twenties:** As psychologist Meg Jay wrote, "This is when leaves turn to trees" and we form lasting views of the world.

- **Ask about your grandparents:** It may open a window into how your parents raised you.

- **Structure your interview to tap into heart, head, and soul:** Once you have a boatload of questions, you can organize them into a three-act structure. Start by asking your parents about stuff they care about—the heart. These are usually *why* questions. Then go to the head. These are *how* questions. If you're in rhythm, you can ask a few *soul* questions at the end. Thanks, Cal Fussman.

- **Record multiple interviews (if you can):** If you get your parents to commit to three interviews, it will allow you to go deeper. With my dad, we spent a whole interview on magic. What's your version of this?

- **(Mostly) conduct interviews one at a time:** This is all about family dynamics. Will your dad monopolize the interview? Do your parents play well off each other? Generally, I recommend going one at a time, but only you can make this call.

- **What's one piece of audio you will want after your parents are gone?:** Poems, recipes, or the exact location of buried treasure. Maybe schedule a twenty-minute interview just for this.

DURING THE INTERVIEW

- **Does anyone need to pee?:** Do it now.

- **Avoid high ceilings and marble floors:** Set up in a room with carpets, couches, or endangered animal hides. They absorb echoes.

- **Car rides ease edginess:** This may surprise you but if you just *barely* mustered the courage to interview your parents, long car rides tend to loosen people up. The audio won't be perfect, but it's better than not doing the interview at all.

- **Keep your friends close and your microphone closer:** Whether you use an iPhone or a professional microphone, keep it no farther than a fist's distance away from the speaker's face. If they're sitting at a table, put your phone on a stack of books, just below their chin.

- **Start with a laugh:** Open with a question that inspires a funny story or a topic they love. Think hobbies, quirks, or passion projects.

- **Don't be married to your questions:** Let curiosity guide the way. If you notice energy around a certain topic, ask a follow-up question.

- **Ask follow-up questions including:** Why? How so? What did that feel like?

- **Pause:** Sit in silence for as long as you need. Slow down the tempo to draw out more depth. What would Werner Herzog do?

- **Show me your hands:** Keep your body language open and friendly. Smile. Nod. Hands on the table.

- **Don't correct them:** Remember, your parents are expressing how they feel about their lives. Facts are secondary. This isn't an interrogation, it's an exploration.

- **Stories are the gas; questions are the brakes:** When steering an interview, stories are the gas, and questions are the brakes. If your guest is shy, you may need to tell a story to infuse more energy into the interview. But if the guest is on a roll, your only job is to listen, pump the brakes, and ask follow-up questions to draw out more detail.

- **Mirroring:** If you want them to be vulnerable, be vulnerable. If you want to crank up the humor, tell a funny story.

- **Difficult topics:** When covering emotionally sensitive material, let them talk for as long as they need. Ask follow-up questions but don't interrupt. You can say things like "Your experience seems really hard" and "What did that feel like?" and "What happened next?" and "Tell me more about [blank]".

- **Limit the interview to two hours or less:** Unless your parents are professional talk show hosts, they will be exhausted after an hour...two at most. I recommend splitting the project into a three-part series.

- **End the interview with a compliment:** Remember the Gottman Ratio? Happy relationships have a five-to-one ratio of positive to negative interactions. Finish the interview with a specific compliment.

AFTER THE INTERVIEW

- **Unwind:** Go on a run. Have a beer. Scream into a pillow. Whatever is called for.

- **Organize the audio:** Rename the audio files clearly with the name, topic, and date.

- **Save the files in multiple places:** Google Drive, Dropbox, or an external hard drive. Make sure someone else knows where they are. You want your great-great-great-great-grandkids to listen to this audio on their morning commute to Mars.

- **Listen on a walk:** A few days after you record, take a stroll and listen to the interview on your phone. New insights will emerge.

- **Journal:** Integration is a core component to any psychedelic experience, and interviewing your parents can feel oddly psychedelic. Prompt yourself with the following questions: What surprised me? Why? How do I feel now? What am I still curious about?

- **Consider removing your voice:** The phone and the Audio-Technica will record only your parents' voices. Your questions will sound like a distant whisper from the closet. And that's okay. I recommend completely cutting yourself out of the interview. Then the final product will sound like a single stream-of-consciousness reflection. Cutting your voice manually in GarageBand will take hours. Descript.com is an AI tool that allows you to import a single audio track, and it will pick up the different voices and transcribe them, one for each speaker. Then you can just delete your lines and export a new audio file, and it will sound as if your parents are flying through a deep monologue.

- **Contact them the next day:** Thank them for the interview. It's easy to feel self-conscious after sharing personal details—let them know you appreciate it.

- **Practice asking questions every day:** These interviews are just the beginning. Practice your question-asking skills in daily conversations. Get good at listening. When we talk, we are limited to the knowledge in our brains, but when we listen, we open the door to infinity.

BONUS QUESTIONS

1. What's the most embarrassing fashion trend you fully committed to?

2. Tell me the story of your first concert.

3. How did you lose your virginity?

4. Who has been your greatest enemy? What's the story?

5. If you could create one universal law, what would it be?

6. Describe your perfect morning.

7. Was there a defining failure early in life that you now see as a gift?

8. Who was your greatest mentor?

9. If you had to disappear for a year, where would you go? Why?

10. If you could gain one skill from someone you admire, what would it be?

11. What always puts you in a good mood?

12. Would you rather live in a world without music or visual art?

13. What do you most value in friendship?

14. If you could give your twenty-year-old self one piece of advice, what would you say?

15. What value do you most hope I carry forward?

My Exact Podcast Setup

IF YOU PLAN ON RECORDING ONLY ONE INTERVIEW, YOU DON'T need to buy the stuff below. But if you want to start a podcast or interview lots of people, this gear is solid. When I launched my podcast in 2017, I iterated dozens of times before I found a setup that worked for me. Fancier stuff exists, but I've optimized my gear for a combination of quality, durability, and mobility. Everything fits in a backpack, so I can record on the road. For links to everything, go to Thiermann.substack.com/gear.

- **Zoom PodTrak P4 ($70)**: This thing rocks. You can record with up to four people and also use it for remote interviews.

- **Pyle Microphones ($20)**: I've had my Pyle microphones for years, and they're still going strong. Get four. They'll last you forever.

- **Foam Mic Cover ($7)**: Get the five-pack. Again with the popping Ps.

- **Audio-Technica ATH-M30x Headphones ($80):** Get at least two. It's an investment, but your ears will thank you later.

- **Portable Charger ($23):** If you don't plug an external charger into your PodTrak P4, you will go through a ton of AA batteries. Any lightweight charger with USB-C port will work fine. I use an external charger whenever I record podcasts.

- **AA Batteries ($18):** I keep a twenty-four pack of batteries in my backpack in case the external charger decides to take the day off. Nothing screams amateur like having your recorder die mid-interview, and needing to ask your guest if they have any batteries lying around.

- **64 GB Memory Card ($30):** Get at least two. If one fills up mid-interview, you can have a backup at the ready. Be sure to format the card every so often so you never run out of space.

- **Three-foot XLR Cables ($20):** These come in a four-pack. Three-foot cables are long enough for you to sit across the table from your guest, but not so long that you feel like you're recording in a pit of snakes.

- **Short USB-C to USB-C ($7):** You need these to plug your external charger into your PodTrak P4, and when plugging your recorder into a computer for remote interviews. One foot is a good length.

- **Portable Microphone Stands ($15):** These are nice so your guest doesn't need to hold the microphone. Okay, that's it. Have fun.

Gratitude

A FRIEND PASSED AWAY THIS YEAR, AND AFTER I HEARD THE news, it took me a week to cry. I just carried on, agitated, incapable of making contact with grief. Then I put pen to paper, and holy shit did I cry.

Writing allows me to access deeper parts of myself, and the people below have helped me inhabit my voice on paper with more fluency and familiarity. Whether through draft reads, designs, or endless edits, each and every one of them has pushed me to become more...*me*. The version of myself that I want to be more like.

First in line is Kendall Strabala, the girl who cuts apples with butter knives, wakes up with entire book plots in her head, and reminds me that love really is all it's cracked up to be. (Pssst... tomorrow I will be proposing to you while on our hike in Big Sur.)

Thank you also to Steve Hawk and Pamm Higgins. When I told you two about this book idea, you served as editors, therapists, and confidants all the way to the finish line. You are my hero couple, and I see your murderous red lines as acts of love. These two saints are joined by Elizabeth Limbach, my first editor at *Santa Cruz Waves* magazine, who nurtured my voice and got me from zero to one. Chris Ryan had a profound influence on my thinking and podcasting style. Thank you for opening doors, teaching me to "question the premise," and for all those nights you let me fart in your Sprinter, Scarlett Jo-van-sson.

To my agent, John Meils, and everyone at DeFiore & Company, thank you for encouraging me to follow my heart with this one, even though I'm sure we could have Frankensteined it into a "Heal-Your-Wounds-in-Six-Minutes-or-Less" book, making it more broadly appealing. Thank you to the team at Scribe Media for embracing this odd duck with open arms, and Anna Dorfman for the cover art. Tremendous.

Although this was a short book, the emotional weight could fill a library. Thank you to my friend, business partner, and wardrobe advisor, Charlie Hart, who always knew the magic words to get me back in the groove: "Let's bike to Will Rogers."

Neil Strauss graciously let me join his writing group and encouraged me not to hide behind vulnerability with glibness. Adam Skolnick for his wisdom, solid advice, and shared love of swimming with juvenile Great White sharks. Shane Heath, for hiring me as a copywriter before I knew what one was—you exemplify true leadership. Scott Norton for showing me that advertising can be a real career, and for teaching me to ask the important question with every creative brief: "What do you want to see more of in the world?"

Thank you to Dersu Rhodes, Chris Keener, Pete Vlastelica, Steven Preisman, Thomas Kemeny, David Littlejohn, Dani Harrison, and everyone at Humanaut for helping me turn pro. You are the best creatives in the biz, and I'm humbled to rub shoulders (and pens) with you.

I'm so proud to have grown up in Santa Cruz. Thank you to the icy water, right-hand point breaks, kelp, sea otters, and redwood trees for being my Home-on-Earth.

Thank you to Kyle Buthman for teaching me how to get barreled (and telling me to interview ET). Chachi for the headshots and for making my surfing look more stylish than it really is. Chris Clemente for always nailing the clip. Tyler Fox and Greg Long for your mentorship in the big stuff. And everyone at Patagonia for your steadfast support over the years.

Writing a book is far from a solitary act. Thank you to the following friends for not blocking me, despite my insanely egoic presumption that you would want to spend your weekends reading *another* draft of my fucking book: Malcolm Fleschner, James Rickman, Sara Russell, Tony Andrews, Dylan Sohngen, Chris Carter, Rick Hanson, Amie Tornincasa, Conrad DeMasi, Dylan Snyder, Kevin Grunewald, Eli Cordell, Zach Schwarzbach, Tighe Melville, and Michael Swamer.

Whew, almost done.

I'd like to thank my family for trusting me with this project. Adele and Rick Carter, Becca and Justin Davis, Toby and Ariel Thiermann, and my two dads: ET and Foster. I love you.

And of course, thank you to Kimberly Jane for modeling courage and showing up in all the ways that matter.

About the Author

An award-winning journalist, pro big wave surfer, and podcast host with more than four hundred episodes, **KYLE THIERMANN** is curiosity in motion. His podcast guests include longevity expert Dr. Peter Attia, 3x Surfing World Champion Mick Fanning, and his own dad—where the idea for this book began.

Kyle has written for *Outside*, *SURFER*, and Discovery Channel, covering indigenous conflicts in Chile and exposing how Hawaii's wild pigs are killing coral. A cultural provocateur at heart, Kyle has spearheaded national advertising campaigns for cult brands including MUD\WTR, Yeti, and Patagonia, crafting billboards above LAX and viral commercials seen by more than one hundred million people.

Earlier, Kyle tried stand-up comedy before realizing that 9:00 p.m. is past his bedtime. At least, that's the story he tells himself.

www.ingramcontent.com/pod-product-compliance
Lightning Source LLC
Chambersburg PA
CBHW030443090526
44586CB00044B/611